Beautiful Light

Beautiful Light, by internationally acclaimed lighting designer Randall Whitehead and lighting industry expert and educator Clifton Stanley Lemon, is an idea book and design guide. It explores the transition in residential lighting from incandescent light sources to LEDs, and how to apply LED lighting with great success.

It begins with the fundamental characteristics of light, including color temperature, color rendering, and spectral power distribution, and how LEDs differ from older light sources. Combining innovative graphics with the enduring design principles of good lighting, the book explains how to design with light layers, light people, and balance daylight and electric light. Every room of the house, as well as exterior and garden spaces, is addressed in 33 case studies of residential lighting with LEDs, with a wide variety of lighting projects in different styles.

Showcasing over 200 color photographs of dramatic interiors beautifully lit with LEDs, and clear, concise descriptions of design strategies and product specifications, *Beautiful Light* helps both professionals and non-professionals successfully navigate the new era of LEDs in residential lighting.

Randall Whitehead is one of the foremost authorities on residential lighting and has written six books on the subject. *Beautiful Light* will be the seventh. His work has appeared in many publications including *Architectural Digest*, *House Beautiful*, *Esquire*, *Horticulture*, and *Architectural Record*. He writes a monthly column for *Furniture, Lighting & Décor* magazine called "The Lighting Doctor" where he discusses lighting trends and addresses lighting dilemmas. He has given presentations for LightFair, LightShowWest, Strategies in Light, the American Society of Interior Designers (ASID), the American Institute of Architects (AIA), the National Kitchen and Bath Association (NKBA), the American Lighting Association (ALA), and the Illuminating Engineering Society (IES). He has also appeared as a guest expert on HGTV, the Discovery Channel, CNN, and Martha Stewart Living Radio.

Clifton Stanley Lemon is CEO of Clifton Lemon Associates, a consultancy providing strategy, marketing, and education services to the lighting and energy industries. He is the Business Development Director for the California Energy Alliance and the Co-Chair of the Strategies in Light conference. He was formerly Marketing Communications Manager for Soraa; Director of Business Development at Integral Group; and founder and CEO of BrandSequence. Clifton is an active writer and speaker and has extensive experience in curricula development for professional training in lighting and energy efficiency. He is a past President of the Illuminating Engineering Society San Francisco Section, and is on the Advisory Board of LightFair International.

Beautiful Light

An Insider's Guide to LED Lighting in Homes and Gardens

Randall Whitehead
Clifton Stanley Lemon

Routledge
Taylor & Francis Group

NEW YORK AND LONDON

First published 2022
by Routledge
605 Third Avenue, New York, NY 10158

and by Routledge
2 Park Square, Milton Park, Abingdon, Oxon, OX14 4RN

Routledge is an imprint of the Taylor & Francis Group, an informa business

© 2022 Randall Whitehead and Clifton Stanley Lemon

The right of Randall Whitehead and Clifton Stanley Lemon to be identified as authors of this work has been asserted by them in accordance with sections 77 and 78 of the Copyright, Designs and Patents Act 1988.

All rights reserved. No part of this book may be reprinted or reproduced or utilised in any form or by any electronic, mechanical, or other means, now known or hereafter invented, including photocopying and recording, or in any information storage or retrieval system, without permission in writing from the publishers.

Trademark notice: Product or corporate names may be trademarks or registered trademarks, and are used only for identification and explanation without intent to infringe.

Library of Congress Cataloging-in-Publication Data
Names: Whitehead, Randall, author. | Lemon, Clifton Stanley, author.
Title: Beautiful Light: an insider's guide to LED lighting in homes and gardens / Randall Whitehead, Clifton Stanley Lemon.
Description: Abingdon, Oxon; New York: Routledge, [2022] | Includes bibliographical references and index.
Identifiers: LCCN 2020051393 (print) | LCCN 2020051394 (ebook) | ISBN 9780367618025 (hardback) | ISBN 9780367618001 (paperback) | ISBN 9781003106616 (ebook)
Subjects: LCSH: Lighting, Architectural and decorative. | Garden lighting. | LED lighting.
Classification: LCC NK2115.5.L5 W469 2021 (print) | LCC NK2115.5.L5 (ebook) | DDC 621.32/2—dc23
LC record available at https://lccn.loc.gov/2020051393
LC ebook reco rd available at https://lccn.loc.gov/2020051394

ISBN: 978-0-367-61802-5 (hbk)
ISBN: 978-0-367-61800-1 (pbk)
ISBN: 978-1-003-10661-6 (ebk)

Typeset in Avenir
by Apex Covantage, LLC

Contents

Foreword	viii
Introduction	1

Part I The Story of Beautiful Light

Overview	8
1. Evolution of Interior Lighting	10
2. LEDS Are Different, and Better	14
3. Qualities of Light	22
4. Lighting People	30
5. Light Layering	34
6. Light, Color, Materials, Finishes, and Food	42
7. Types of Lamps and Luminaires	48
8. Control Issues	56
9. Designing Sustainably	60
10. The Design Process	64
11. Typical Lighting Fails	68

Part II Interior Lighting

Overview	78
12. Kitchens	80
Project 1	84
Project 2	86
Project 3	88
Project 4	90
13. Bathrooms	94
Project 1	98
Project 2	100

Project 3	102
Project 4	104

14. Living Rooms — 108

Project 1	112
Project 2	114
Project 3	116
Project 4	118

15. Dining Rooms — 122

Project 1	128
Project 2	130
Project 3	132
Project 4	134

16. Bedrooms — 138

Project 1	142
Project 2	144
Project 3	146
Project 4	148

17. Entries — 152

Project 1	156
Project 2	158
Project 3	162
Project 4	164

18. Open Plan Spaces — 168

Project 1	172
Project 2	174
Project 3	176
Project 4	178

Part III Exterior Lighting

Overview	184

19. Exterior Spaces — 186

Project 1	192
Project 2	196
Project 3	198
Project 4	200
Project 5	202

Part IV Design Details

20. Design Details — 208

Lighting Ceilings	210
Cove Lighting	211

Wall Washing	212
Wall Grazing	212
Under-cabinet Lighting	213
Pendants and Decorative Lighting	213
Skylights and Daylighting	214
Downlights	215
Vanity Lighting	215
Exterior Area and Security Lighting	216
Landscape Lighting	216
Path and Step Lights	217

Part V Resources

Glossary of Lighting Terms	220
Bibliography	226
Acknowledgments	228
Index	229

Foreword

We wrote this book in order to help designers, architects, and homeowners improve the lighting of their residential and landscape projects by sharing the techniques of well-integrated lighting design and light layering.

Even though for the past ten years or so we have gotten used to the exciting new technology for lighting – Light Emitting Diodes (LEDs) – the fundamental principles of good lighting haven't changed. What's happened instead is that LEDs, when selected and used correctly, can do everything incandescents could do even but better, while saving energy and lasting longer. They even allow us to do new fabulous things with light we never imagined before.

This is a learning look-book. We begin by showing you the principles of good lighting design, and even some examples of what not to do, then provide profiles of residential projects in different styles. In each of these we explain how the look was accomplished, what components were used to create the effects, and how the different layers of light interact to create Beautiful Light.

Introduction

The basic premise of Beautiful Light is threefold: first, we explain the transition in residential lighting that's taken place over the last fifteen years or so – from incandescent light sources to LEDs (light emitting diodes) Second, we provide some grounding in the fundamental qualities of light as they relate to residential lighting. And third, we will show how LEDs can be applied with great success, following the enduring design principles of good lighting.

The transition from incandescent and fluorescent lighting to LEDs was relatively rapid, but it's notable in that it was the first such change in technology since fluorescent light sources emerged in the 1940s. The incandescent lightbulb was invented and brought into widespread use in the late nineteenth and early twentieth centuries, and fluorescent light sources did not see the wide adoption in residential use that was expected, due to poor light quality. In essence lighting innovation has been extremely slow in terms of the pace of innovation technology compared to almost every other area of technology in the past century or so. Another notable characteristic of the LED revolution is that the shift in energy efficiency from incandescent lightbulbs to LEDs has been dramatic – on average, energy use for lighting has dropped to less that 20% of what it was before LEDs. This is largely a success story, because while early LED products were of poor quality, mature LED products now offer not just equal, but better quality than fluorescent and incandescent light sources. They also bring many other benefits, including longer lifetimes, flexibility, and affordability.

Beautiful Light is a practical guide to interior and exterior residential lighting, focusing on our combined understanding of the basic art and craft of residential lighting design, developed from over four decades of professional design practice – in Randall's case lighting design and writing, and in Clifton's multidisciplinary design, writing, and education. The two of us have collaborated on lighting books for many years. We don't claim to present the definitive theory for or approach to residential lighting – the field of lighting design is still young, and there are many true masters of lighting design all over the world (several of whom we count as dear friends and colleagues), with their own styles and finely honed practices. We do share with most of the best practitioners the belief in a well-balanced layering of light from various sources to shape spaces in the built environment, give them meaning, and make them inviting, nurturing, sustainable, and safe. Some designers may refer to what we call "light layering" by different terms, postulate more or fewer layers, or offer varying approaches. Many of today's lighting designers also believe in lighting people first, although this is less common. Randall has always been one of the leading proponents of this approach, probably because of his origins as a photographer, an art form where lighting faces correctly is crucial to success. We think of this as the original "human centric" lighting.

Our book is not meant to be a detailed technical manual for electrical engineering, lighting calculations, or lighting controls, as there are many excellent sources for this information, some of which are listed in the bibliography. We do provide an index of useful technical design and installation details used in many of the projects. We focus on residential lighting design, as this comprises Randall's main expertise, and applies to an increasing variety of building types, including multifamily structures. But we don't cover commercial or industrial lighting – there are many excellent sources that focus on these applications. We also do not delve too deeply into the more theoretical aspects of light and lighting, as this direction is a path that is long, fascinating, and complex – but still tangential to a working understanding of basic craft. The more you learn about the physics and science of light, color, perception, and behavior, the more you realize that each is a main branch in the trunk of knowledge, and worthy of entire research disciplines. With all the different technical developments and advancements in myriad scientific fields, in many ways we're just at the beginning of understanding the interrelationships between light, color, biological processes, and behavior. We cannot even begin to claim a deep understanding of, for instance, circadian processes, quantum physics, and neuroscience – all, by the way, fields eagerly embraced by many leading innovators in the lighting industry.

Beautiful Light is intended for an audience with one thing in common – the need to understand how to use LEDs in residential lighting following the time-honored design principles of light layering and lighting people. Within this purview are three basic groups – students, practicing design professionals, and homeowners. For students, most design programs in educational institutions today don't yet include much in the way of lighting courses, and it's fairly typical for those studying interior design, architecture, landscape design, or electrical engineering to be offered only one or two courses on the subject in their entire course of study: this book is intended to serve as a resource for these kinds of courses. For practicing design professionals, including lighting designers, *Beautiful Light* is a fundamental introduction to residential lighting design and a source of new ideas. For homeowners, the book will serve as a strong introduction, an idea book, and a guide to working with design professionals or for doing your own design and installation to the extent that you are comfortable and capable.

A few notes on terminology we use throughout the book are in order here. When referring to fixtures and lightbulbs we use the industry insider terms "luminaire" for fixture and "lamp" for lightbulb, unless we're talking about a floor lamp or bedside lamp. Most LEDs are not bulbs at all, and only imitate incandescent forms so they can fit in existing luminaires originally intended for incandescent bulbs. When we refer to the old-fashioned non-LED light sources (except for CFLs, compact fluorescents, which in our opinion have no real place in good residential lighting), which are all lightbulbs, we use the terms "incandescents" and "halogen," which is a specialized form of incandescent bulb. When we refer to color rendering we do not as a rule use the term CRI (Color Rendering Index) exclusively, as there are

▶ Figure INT.1

Photo and Lighting Design: Randall Whitehead.

now metrics for color rendering that differ significantly from CRI, although CRI is still the standard term for most lighting designers, and manufacturers. When referring to electrical power we use V for volts and W for Watts, as in 12V, 75W. When referring to color temperature we often use CCT (for Correlated Color Temperature), and express the measurement with the number followed by K, as in 2700K, where K is understood as "degrees Kelvin."

We limit our theoretical approach more to aesthetic, cultural, behavioral, and historical considerations. We know from long experience what people in residential settings prefer, how they are inclined to behave, and what makes them look and feel their best.

Randall Whitehead
Clifton Stanley Lemon

▶ Figure INT.2

Photo and Lighting Design: Randall Whitehead.

Part I | The Story of Beautiful Light

Overview

This section is the story of how we've come to integrate the relatively new technology of solid state lighting (LEDs) into our traditional design practice of architecture, interior, and lighting design. While the transition from incandescents and fluorescents to LEDs has not been without bumps in the road, we show how it's possible to strike a beautiful balance between natural daylight and electric light in residential design today, and that LEDs are perfectly suited to the task – in many, if not most, ways they're superior to the older lighting technologies.

It's true that technology never seems to want to stop evolving, and we will certainly see more improvements to LEDs. But for now we're no longer in the adoption phase of the technology where we're waiting for high quality products to become affordable or practical. Many of the advances in the near future are likely to be incremental rather than revolutionary, and this is not a bad thing. Designers as craftspeople need time to get used to their tools stabilizing so that they can develop best practices.

A key idea in our understanding and practice of residential lighting design, and one that we repeat many times in this book, is the focus on lighting people and skin. The location in the home where this is most critical is in the bathroom, at the vanity. Architects and interior designers don't have much control over their clients, the human beings who inhabit the spaces they design, so they care mostly about the things they do control – the materials, finishes, furniture, and colors in the environment. Subsequently lighting designers, who are largely following the lead of architects and interior designers, often forget about lighting people. Truly human-centric design is a holistic process of making people look better throughout the day and into the evening, not only at the vanity, but in all rooms of the house, in the context of fabrics, furniture, food, finishes, and materials.

In this section we review the basic properties of light and the techniques and tools in the lighting designer's palette: light layering; types of lamps and luminaires; controls. We also talk about how to do this sustainably and as part of an integrated and collaborative design team.

Finally, we've learned that studying lighting fails is one of the best ways to learn to "see" and create good residential lighting, and we provide many very typical examples of lighting as an afterthought to what is often very good residential design. Once you've learned to identify the common mistakes, you'll be in a much better position to transform your clients' (and your own) spaces with beautiful light.

▶ Figure SBLO.1

Photo and Lighting Design: Randall Whitehead.

Chapter 1

Evolution of Interior Lighting

In order to explore the evolution of lighting in the home we start with a brief examination of our modern Western concept of the home, the archetypal structures that embody it, and how they evolved. Even though the ideas of family and, indeed, "home" are fluid social and cultural constructs and are constantly shaped by the combined forces of technology, economics, and urbanization, for the purpose of focusing our discussion to perhaps the most commonly understood model in the United States today, we'll talk about the single-family home. Whether single- or multi-story with detached walls on a separate plot of land or as part of a larger multi-family building, this layout is typically comprised of a collection of single purpose rooms – living room, dining room, kitchen, bedrooms, bathrooms, multipurpose open plan rooms, miscellaneous utility roms, and outdoor spaces. This particular arrangement has not been the norm for the majority of human history.

The most primeval dwellings made use of shelter to mitigate, and harness, the effects of the environment. Our basic physiological needs demand a roof over our heads and walls to create an envelope for protection from the elements, predators, and enemies and a place for fire, gathering, and preparing and consuming food. A completely dark enclosure is not useful. One of the earliest innovations was an opening in the top of a hut, tipi, or other enclosure that not only let in daylight but allowed for the exhaust of smoke and fumes from the cooking fire and oil lamps which were necessary to dispel the darkness.

Before advanced lighting technology (candles, gas lamps, then electric lights) humans evolved under conditions of light that centered around the daily rhythms of sunlight during the day and firelight at night. It's easy to imagine that our visual equipment –our eyes and brain – are hardwired for these two conditions and the transitions between them. Indeed, vision science has identified parts of the eye – rods and cones – that process light at different levels. There are three kinds of vision: scotopic vision, or night vision, which uses only rods to see (objects are visible, but appear in black and white); photopic vision, or daytime vision, which uses cones and provides color; and mesopic vision, the in-between vision, which we use most of the time in mid-level light conditions.

As tribal groups grew in size and complexity, communal dwellings evolved that were organized around a central fire. People all slept in the same large lodge or room, along with the dogs. Light was provided by oil lamps, fire, and openings which were often no more than holes in walls or ceilings that let in light and air and allowed smoke to escape.

▲Figure 1.1

Four stages of complexity in the evolution of interior lighting: 1. Sky light and firelight in a primitive hut. 2. Sky light and firelight in a log cabin with small windows. 3. Single source ceiling lighting in a modern home. 4. Balanced layers of light: ambient, task, accent, and decorative. Illustration: Clifton Stanley Lemon.

Our current arrangement of single purpose rooms seems to have begun in 12th century Northern Europe with the innovation of the chimney. This was the era of a mini Ice Age, and temperatures were much colder than what we're experiencing today. Chimneys allowed multi-story buildings to share distributed heat from one shaft. This hastened the development of smaller rooms which were more economical to heat, which contributed to the modern idea of domestic privacy – a "room of one's own," so to speak. Windows in these buildings were expensive and were sometimes glazed with thin sheets of animal horn, a material also used for lanterns.

The ancient Romans had developed advanced glass manufacturing methods that made glass windowpanes affordable for many buildings by 200 CE, but this technology was lost during the Dark Ages between 400 and 800 CE. In the 14th century however, French glassmakers perfected the technology of making flat panes of transparent glass, which were initially small and required assembly in lattices or window frames. Gradually window openings became larger and allowed buildings to make more use of daylight. Before gas and then electric light, an architectural tradition had developed that made skillful use of buildings' volume, surfaces, and windows to modulate daylight for lighting the home. In fact, an archaic architectural term for windows is "lights."

At night though, interior lighting for most homes consisted of fires, candles, and eventually more sophisticated lamps using oil and kerosene. The next lighting technology revolution was gas lamps, which produced a much brighter light and began to dispel darkness at sufficient levels to extend working hours and, along with many other rapidly evolving technologies, impact forms of social organization and family structure. Ingenious devices were invented that multiplied the fragile, precious light as much as possible – chandeliers for instance were devised to amplify candlelight and were a great status symbol as only rich people could afford candles in medieval times. The forms of these luminaires persisted long after fossil fuel-based lighting gave way to electric lighting. Also, all fuel-based lighting produced noxious, unhealthy fumes and coated interior surfaces (and lungs) with soot and other chemical deposits.

When electricity as a distributed power source emerged in the 19th and early 20th centuries, electric lighting was the first application of this groundbreaking new technology. The cost and effort involved in running power lines from the local coal gas burning power plant to the home meant that typically only one light per room was feasible, and it was placed in the center of the room in the ceiling. This remains a default lighting strategy in many homes today, even though it's entirely inadequate for providing a well-lighted environment.

As electric lighting expanded and became ubiquitous in residential use throughout the 20th century, the modern practice of lighting design was born, exemplified by designers like Richard Kelly, who articulated the theory of light layers. Even though electric incandescent light had technical limitations we no longer have today with LEDs, designers like Kelly established a solid methodology that involves identifying the various purposes for types of lighting and blending them carefully into an integrated whole.

What LEDs have done is allow us to use the light layering approach to much greater advantage, with better light that is much more efficient, lasts longer, and can be applied easily in more locations than ever before. It also allows us to improve lighting so that people look and feel better – this is the most important benefit of beautiful light with LEDs.

▲ Figure 1.2

This home shows a well calibrated balance between cooler daylight and warmer electric light in ambient, accent, and decorative layers. Photo: Dennis Anderson, Lighting Design: Randall Whitehead.

▲ Figure 1.3

What we call the skyline/fire line theory of lighting says that humans evolved to see brighter, cooler ambient light (sky light) from above and warmer light (firelight) from below. Photos: Clifton Stanley Lemon.

CHAPTER 1 Evolution of Interior Lighting 13

Chapter 2

LEDs Are Different, and Better

When LEDs were first introduced, it was hard for us to part with our old friends incandescent and halogen lamps, and the luminaires made for them. It seemed like nothing could ever replace the warm glow, beautiful color rendering, and tight beam patterns of lamps like the MR16 and PAR. But incandescent light sources are unacceptably inefficient – 95% of the output of a typical incandescent lightbulb is in the non-visible infrared spectrum, which is to say, heat. Compact fluorescents (CFLs) are considerably more efficient than incandescents, but never quite made it into widespread residential use, mostly for poor quality of light reasons.

LEDs were originally developed to be much more efficient, a crucial need in our world today, and they succeeded. Unfortunately, as with any new technology, early versions of LEDs were inadequate in many ways – especially color rendering – and much product was released on the market which was not quite suitable for home use. But these growing pains subsided gradually, and subsequent generations of LED lighting products eventually emerged that are truly better than incandescents in every significant way: efficiency, longevity, color rendering, distribution, flexibility, and thermal performance.

It's natural for us to compare LEDs to incandescents and halogens (a type of incandescent with a small amount of halogen gas in the bulb), since the hot lightbulbs we all grew up with had been the dominant lighting technology for well over a century until LEDs evolved. But while much of the effort to ensure adoption of LEDs has focused on making them as much like incandescents as possible, LEDs are fundamentally different, and to work with them in residential lighting design you need to understand the differences between the two technologies, as well as the similarities.

Energy Efficiency

On average, LEDs use only 20% of the energy of incandescent lamps, which still make up the majority of installed residential light sources. One key difference with LEDs is that we measure their energy use by lumens per Watt (or lm/W) rather than Watts only. This is the "miles per gallon" measurement for lighting, and is an improvement over Watts only because it focuses on the output (what we're getting for the energy used) rather than the input only—you would never refer to a car as a "25 gallon vehicle." It's also different because the efficiency of incandescents never varied too much, so our idea of brightness used to be, and in many cases still is, gauged by Watts. Not so with LEDS—the measure of brightness is lumens—you can almost always find this metric on the package. Typical lumens per Watt in commercially available LEDs today ranges between 80 and 200. Some states in the U.S. have established minimum efficiency requirements for light sources: California's Title 20 for instance requires a minimum 80lm/W. We feel that LEDs on the market now are sufficiently efficient, and while efficiency is and will always be important, we no longer need to sacrifice light quality for efficiency like we did when LEDs were first introduced.

Form

It's important to remember that LEDs are not actually "bulbs" in the sense that incandescent light sources are. They make light in a completely different way, as explained below, but only take on the form of incandescent bulbs in order to fit into luminaires designed for incandescents, not because the form is required for LEDs to work properly. This makes LEDs more comprehensible and adaptable, as they can be used in older luminaires. Then again, many LED light sources have no need to use older forms of luminiares, as they're thinner, lighter, cooler, smaller, and more powerful. In fact, because of the pace of change, most designers of lighting equipment have not quite yet begun to explore the full possibilities of new forms for LEDs. We're still in a transition period between the old technology and the new, and probably will be for many years.

Longevity and Maintenance

LEDs last much longer than incandescent and halogen light sources and can save time and money in replacement and maintenance costs. LEDs fail by gradually losing their light output: this is what is measured by the metric "lumen maintenance." Don't trust lifetime claims over 60K hours. Alex Baker, who heads government affairs and public policy efforts for the Illuminating Engineering Society (IES), has done extensive research into lighting manufacturers' claims of long lifetime claims for this products and demonstrated that most are simply not supported by evidence beyond that threshold.

Flexibility and Size

High output LEDs can be tiny –a fraction of the size of equivalent incandescents – and can fit anywhere. LED linear lights, for instance, are incredibly flexible and can provide illumination in many places that were previously difficult or impossible to light.

Thermal Performance

LEDs are generally considerably cooler than incandescent lights but still generate heat. LEDS are also much more sensitive to thermal conditions – if you are replacing halogen lamps with LEDs in enclosed fixtures, check specifications on box or cutsheets to make sure the product is rated for enclosed fixtures.

Color Rendering

The best LEDs on the market today provide color rendering that is equal to or better than halogen sources, but in a different way. As we look more closely at color rendering, we see that even incandescent sources, long considered the gold standard for color rendering, are not perfect. Also, the metric commonly used for measuring color rendering, CRI, is far from perfect, as it's possible to find light sources with an acceptable or even a high CRI of over 90 with poor color rendering. Color rendering is a complex phenomenon, and probably the hardest to get used to with LEDs – the way they produce light and render color is fundamentally different than previous light sources, but at their best they're better than incandescent.

Color Temperature and Tunable Color

It's possible to create LEDs with any conceivable color temperature, the range is unlimited. For residential lighting though, we need a relatively narrow range, from 2200K at the lowest to 4000K at the coolest.

One aspect of LEDs is completely new and different – color tuning. In addition to dimming, LEDS can change CCT. This has never been possible before outside of theater and photography lighting. We are simply not quite used to this yet, as all previous light sources had fixed CCTs. But now that we have it, we're really making the best of it in many situations, practical or otherwise. For instance, previewing our clothing choices in our closet is a convenient application of tunable LED lighting.

▼ Figure 2.1

This closet light uses tunable white linear LEDs to allow you to pick your outfit under conditions that imitate day or night conditions. On the left, when you're getting dressed in the morning, a cooler temperature shows the appearance of your clothes under daylight. On the right, a warm color temperature shows their appearance in the evening. Photo: Randall Whitehead.

There are three basic types of color tunable LED lights – warm dim, tunable white, and full color tunable. This capability is accomplished by using various combinations of different color "emitters" within the LED chips that can be combined in varying percentages. Warm dim color tuning imitates incandescent behavior and makes an LED warmer in CCT when dimmed. Tunable white produces you a range of colors typically between a cool CCT such as 4000K and a warm one such as 2400K. Some are available that go as high as 5000K and as low as 2150K. These are very useful in that closet, as shown in Figure 2.1, or an open plan layout where the kitchen is seen from the living and dining areas. You can use cooler light in the kitchen for doing food prep, then change to warmer light for eating or entertaining. Full color tunable lamps and luminaires can produce thousands of colors, including rich warm whites, peachy pink, or cornflower blue. Generally this capability is used for special events like parties, but since it's so new, and there are many lighting products on the market that allow full color tuning, people are experimenting and having fun. If you prefer a cornflower blue living room when you listen to Black Sabbath, you have our full permission to indulge!

▲ Figure 2.2

Full color tunable LED linear lighting livens up this entry. Photo: Dennis Anderson. Lighting Design: Randall Whitehead.

Dimming and Warm Dimming

This is one area where LEDs are very different from incandescents. Because incandescents work on the simple principle of electric resistance, all of them can dim when controlled by sockets that can dim, and all of them will become warmer in CCT when dimmed. LEDs don't inherently operate this way because of how they're controlled – they need specific power supplies or drivers. Not every LED light source can dim and most are not yet "warm dim" capable. And most lighting designers have found that LEDs dimmed down significantly without warm dim capability look washed out. Although warm dim capability has only been introduced in the past five years or so, it's already very good and widely available. Dimming controls are only useful in rooms in the home where you need to change light levels frequently, but that covers many room types, so for residential use, you will probably want LEDs that are warm dim capable.

Distribution

In order to design effectively with LEDs, it's important to understand the fundamentally different way in which they distribute light. Incandescent (and fluorescent) light sources are fundamentally omnidirectional – light from them goes in all directions and must be controlled and directed through often elaborate systems of optics (lenses) and shading devices. This means that even at very low output levels, they require shading and blocking to control the direction of light and mitigate glare, as even a candle in a dark room produces glare and often must be shaded to be used more effectively.

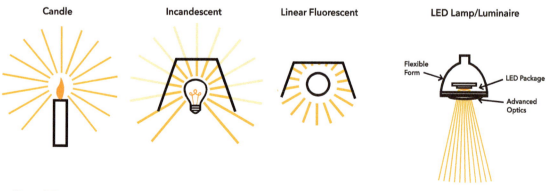

▲ Figure 2.3

Unlike all previous light sources, LED devices are typically inherently directional, which means they're much easier to control in addition to being energy efficient. They don't always require shading and shielding, and often rely only on small, bright, efficient chips and advanced optics to produce very clean beams. Illustration: Clifton Stanley Lemon.

▲ Figure 2.4

Illustration: Clifton Stanley Lemon.

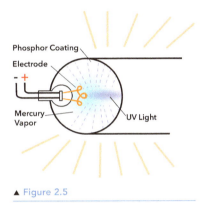

▲ Figure 2.5

Illustration: Clifton Stanley Lemon.

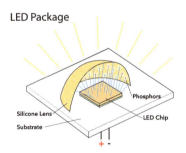

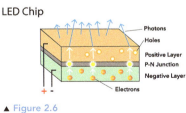

▲ Figure 2.6

Illustration: Clifton Stanley Lemon.

How Incandescents Produce Light

An incandescent light source is basically controlled fire on display. Think of a piece of iron heated in a forge by a blacksmith: as it gets hotter it progresses from black in color to dull red to glowing orange to white hot. Incandescents do the same thing using electrical resistance. When connected between a positive terminal and a negative one, the tungsten filament heats up and gets brighter as it gets hotter.

How Fluorescents Produce Light

Fluorescent lamps are essentially tubes that contain low-pressure mercury-vapor gas and electrodes that use fluorescence to produce visible light. Electric current passes between the electrodes, exciting the mercury vapor, which produces short-wave ultraviolet light that then causes a phosphor coating on the inside of the lamp to glow. Fluorescents are similar to LEDs in that they use short wavelength light to excite phosphors to create white light (they use ultraviolet light while LEDs typically use violet or blue light).

How LEDs Produce Light

While incandescent technology is quite simple, and fluorescent a bit more complex, LEDs are more difficult to explain without delving into quantum physics, which most people think only serious brainiacs understand (actually one of the founders of Quantum Theory, Albert Einstein, admitted he didn't fully understand them either, so that doesn't help!). One place to start is to think of them as reverse solar panels, which convert light to electricity – LEDs just do the opposite, and share underlying technology with solar panels. The following is all still magic, and more than you probably need to know, but here goes …

An LED is a diode, a semiconductor device that essentially acts as a one-way switch for current. It's a special kind of diode, a light emitting diode, or LED. When current is applied to the diode (also called a "chip" like a computer chip), free electrons in one layer of the diode recombine with holes in another layer (called quantum wells) and release energy in the form of light.

The LED chip itself only produces a blue or violet light. In order to make full spectrum white light, the chip is typically encased in a dot of silicone impregnated with a specific phosphor mix. It looks rather like a tiny hummingbird egg yolk. As the phosphors – which are usually green, red, and sometimes blue – react to the violet or blue light they glow, producing white light, similar to how the fluorescent tube works.

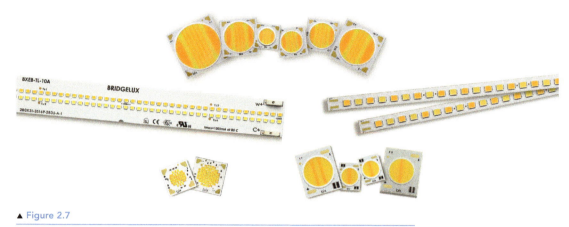

▲ Figure 2.7

Typical LED components: linear and chips. Photo: Bridgelux.

Chapter 3

Qualities of Light

Architects, designers, engineers, contractors, and craftspeople think in tangible physical terms about materials, spaces, and how they interact in assemblies. They also think about the psychological and emotional effects of design when creating the experience of a safe, healthy, beautiful enclosure – the building "envelope." Light is different than wood, concrete, steel, fabric, glass, or leather as it's an ephemeral and mysterious element that's invisible in itself and only exists when it reflects off objects. But it also has an undeniably visceral physical presence, one that literally "renders" all other materials and spaces visible and hence usable. In fact, many architects and designers think of it as a primary "material." Light has one defining quality though – even when distribution is controlled very tightly, it doesn't have sharply defined edges like glass, steel, or stone, but is intrinsically soft and blendable. You can think of it like brushes and paint on a canvas – indeed, when creating Photoshop renderings of lighting schemes, you often use brush tools to achieve the intended effects.

A good working knowledge of the properties of light and how it behaves necessarily includes an understanding of how it affects the human beings living and working in the buildings we design. Good lighting designers care deeply about how light affects vision, perception, cognition, and emotions. An understanding of the basic physical properties of light will guide you when applying the theory of light layering and color theory and help you to select and specify equipment – lamps, luminaires, and controls. Becoming a well-rounded designer means having a grasp of these concepts both in theory and in practice. These basic qualities of light are intensity, distribution, direction, color (which includes both color temperature and color rendering), and movement. The lighting designer's tools are organized in these categories.

Intensity

Intensity is basically brightness – a highly quantifiable attribute measured by various metrics including lumens, footcandles, candela, center beam candle power, and lux. For detailed definitions of all these terms, please refer to the Glossary. For purposes of specifying lamps and luminaires, you care about lumens (total output), and when measuring the amount of light that falls where you want it (or not), you care about lux or footcandles. While inherently quantifiable, in practice brightness is relative and has to be understood in context because of how our eyes adjust to light levels. For instance, in a totally dark room, even a candle with very low lumen output is bright and glary, which is why we soften it with shades that diffuse the glow. In another situation, say a room with bright indirect daylight, additional and very bright lighting is sometimes needed to make darker parts of the room visible because our eyes adjust to the brightest light in our field of vision, in this case, daylight.

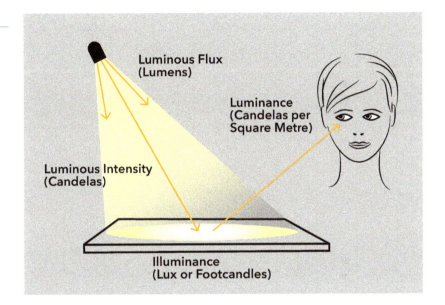

▶ Figure 3.1

The different types of intensity in light. Illustration: Clifton Stanley Lemon.

Distribution

"By means of controlling the distribution of light and creating patterns and compositions of light and shade, it is possible to produce sensations on the retina that will be interpreted as forms in space" (*A Syllabus of Stage Lighting*, S. McCandless 1964). Distribution means the "form" that light takes, which like color is something of a metaphor as light doesn't really have "shape" that we perceive directly. Yet when we design with light, we do come to feel its physicality as having a certain kind of volume.

For practical considerations, the distribution of light sources is one of the important qualities you must consider when specifying lamps or luminaires. As explained in Chapter 2, LEDs are inherently directional light sources, except for forms, like A-lamps, in which LED technology has been used to replicate omnidirectional incandescent sources.

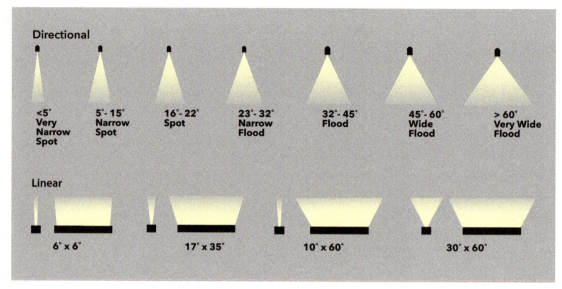

▲ Figure 3.2

Top: common beam angles available in directional LED lamps and luminaires. Bottom: some possible combinations of lateral and throw angles in linear LEDs. A very wide range of beam angle combinations is available from manufacturers today. Illustration: Clifton Stanley Lemon.

Direction

All light has direction, and the lighting designer must choose carefully when placing light sources so that glare and unwanted reflections off surfaces are avoided, and so that colors are rendered appropriately. We expect ambient light to come from above generally, like skylight, and task and accent light to meet us at eye level or below. The effects of lighting on faces are particularly important, as explained in Chapter 4 on lighting people. Cross-illumination from two directions can fill unflattering shadows and give shape to a face lit with flat frontal lighting.

Color Temperature

The "color" of light is also a metaphor that is misleading because light itself has no color. Color is produced by light reflecting off objects. There are two separate aspects of color in light that are relevant to lighting design: color temperature and color rendering. Color temperature, also called "correlated color temperature" or CCT, ranges from warm to cool, along the "blackbody curve," an idealized standard measure of thermal electromagnetic radiation that is similar to the blacksmith's color chart used to gauge the melting temperature of steel.

▶ Figure 3.3

Photo: Needpix.com.

Correlated color temperature, or CCT, indicates the apparent relative warmth or coolness of light. CCT is measured in Kelvin, a temperature scale devised by the British inventor and scientist William Thomson, Lord Kelvin. It is used to indicate not only the "temperature" of light (as explained above in reference to the blacksmith's color chart) but of other materials. Most people don't understand different color temperatures in residential lighting, because before LEDs, incandescent was the primary light source, and it has a fairly limited color range. If they pay any attention to light at all, (many people don't) consumers are familiar with labels on lighting product packaging that indicate warm white, daylight, or cool white.

▲ Figure 3.4

The Lighting Facts label (now discontinued) was similar to the Nutrition Facts label for food, and introduced consumers to the concept of efficiency and color temperature in lamps. Most manufacturers now provide this information on packaging for consumer lighting products, typically listing CCT but not color rendering. Image: Wikimedia Commons.

CHAPTER 3 Qualities of Light   25

In fact the CCT of light spans an extremely wide range. It's possible to make LEDs now in almost any color temperature, but for residential lighting purposes, only the range between 2200K and 4000K are appropriate.

▼ Figure 3.5

Useful range of CCT. Illustration: Clifton Stanley Lemon.

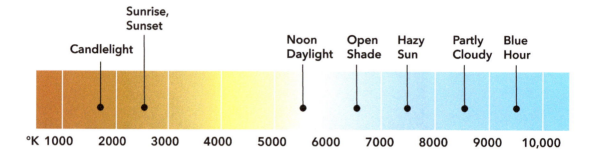

Color Rendering

Color Rendering Index (CRI)

Color rendering is the measurement of how closely a light source renders color compared to a standard reference light source. The first system devised to measure color rendering was developed in 1974 and is called the Color Rendering Index or CRI. The theory behind it is that a light source's ability to render color should be judged by how accurately it renders an arbitrarily chosen set of colors compared to a "reference illuminant" or "standard illuminant" established by the International Commission on Illumination, or the Commision Internationale de l'Eclairage (CIE) in the 1930s. CRI became important when fluorescent light sources were introduced, as they had poor color quality at first and were necessarily judged by how well they imitated both daylight and incandescent light. Although it is no longer a particularly accurate way to define color rendering, it remains the standard reference point for most lighting designers and lighting manufacturers.

▼ Figure 3.6

A typical CRI chart for a light source. Illustration: Clifton Stanley Lemon.

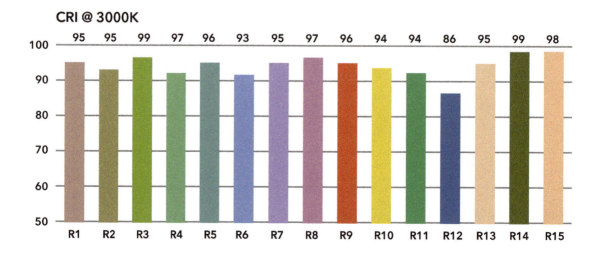

26   PART I The Story of Beautiful Light

TM-30

▼Figure 3.7

Two TM-30 charts showing variation of two 2700K LED light sources. The source on the left has a lower fidelity and gamut score than the source on the right, which means that the higher score renders colors better. Image courtesy of Bridgelux.

With the introduction of LEDs came the ability to create light sources with any desired spectral power distribution, and we realized that a more accurate metric for color rendering was required. The Illuminating Engineering Society put forth the metric as a standard in 2015 – its name TM-30 is an abbreviation of TM-30-18, which stands for Technical Memorandum 30. The theory behind TM-30 is that more reference colors were needed to judge a light source against the reference illuminant, so another somewhat arbitrary set of 99 colors was chosen to use for comparison. TM-30 also added two measurements, Rf for fidelity and Rg for gamut. It represents a definite improvement over CRI, but as of this writing has not replaced CRI, as specifiers and manufacturers prefer a single number to represent color rendering, even though most understand that that may not be entirely sufficient.

▶ Figure 3.8

The most recently introduced metric for color rendering is called Average Spectral Difference or ASD. The graph shows comparative spectral power distribution of five different light sources against a reference illuminant (natural light). Developed and introduced by the LED chip manufacturer Bridgelux in 2020, it calculates color rendering as a function of the average difference of between the spectral power distribution of a light source's compared to the reference illuminant. Unlike CRI and TM-30, lower numbers are better. This new metric shows promise but is not in widespread use yet. Image courtesy of Bridgelux.

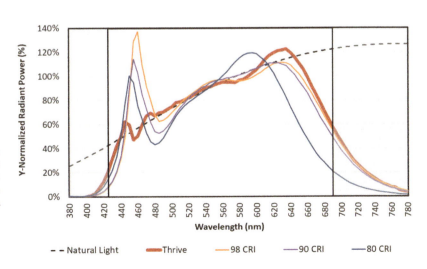

CHAPTER 3 Qualities of Light

Color rendering is often thought of as being "subjective," because it's been very difficult to agree on quality of light ever since electric light was invented. The metrics presented above are only three of perhaps dozens of systems devised to categorize how light sources render color. They do provide a useful way to separate out the good light sources from the bad ones, so that you can spend more time narrowing down what you have to test in person, because that's the only way to really tell if an LED light source will work for your project. When in doubt, test it on yourself – if your hand looks good under the light, your clients probably will too.

▶ Figure 3.10

Sunlight shining through trees produces a beautiful, gently moving light. Photo: Paul Bush/Depositphotos.com.

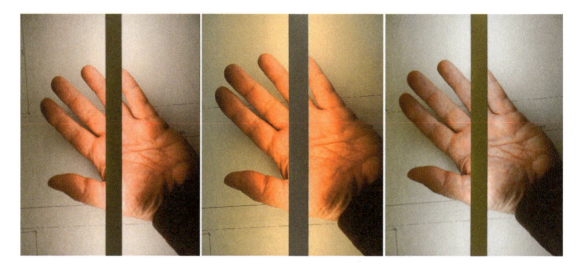

Movement

Movement in light refers to changes in intensity, color, distribution, or direction. Dynamic changes in all of these qualities take place in nature on a regular basis. For instance, the color of daylight changes significantly during the day, or even from one minute to the next, depending on what the clouds are doing. Movement may also include the physical movement of a source, such as a search light, police beacon, color wheel, special optical effect, moving projections, mirror ball, etc.

For most purposes in residential lighting design however, movement should never be rapid or noticeable.

The dappled light filtering down through trees has a gentle, relaxing movement that can be employed in outdoor lighting with the "moonlighting" effect.

▲ Figure 3.9

The best way to see if you like a light source is to test it on your skin. Photo: Randall Whitehead.

▶ Figure 3.11

The same effect at night using LEDs with a filter. Photo courtesy of Beachside Lighting.

Chapter 4

Lighting People

We believe that our first principle of residential lighting – lighting people – is the real "human centric lighting." It's not only about how light makes you feel but about how it makes you look (of course the two are obviously connected). But we are definitely in the minority – most people, including lighting designers, architects, interior designers, and homeowners, only conceive of lighting as something that illuminates furniture, art, finishes, and materials – all the stuff we are keen to show off in order to demonstrate our exquisite taste and confer status! The best designers have an intuitive understanding of the fact that for better or (usually) for worse, the need for status trumps almost all other human drives. This frequently results in poor quality lighting that can ruin an otherwise beautiful architectural, interior, or landscape design.

Few lighting designers today are trained from the beginning in lighting design, as the profession is relatively young and does not yet have a large academic infrastructure behind it. Most study architecture, engineering, and theatrical design, and a few study photography. It's the designers with theatrical or photography backgrounds that best understand lighting people. Many top lighting designers consider Stanley McCandless to be the father of modern lighting design and have been strongly influenced by his work, which includes one of the seminal works on the theory of stage lighting. Many valuable lighting lessons come from the theatrical tradition, where the actor's ability to communicate emotion relies strongly on the face.

The effects of lighting on people are almost never considered by architects and interior designers. Single source lighting is dramatic for lighting objects but is not flattering for faces. Harsh shadows distort the face and can make people look scary or unfriendly, even when they're not, as in the first example in Fig. 4.1 with downlights only, unfortunately a "default" condition favored by architects as fixtures are recessed into the ceiling and preserve the clean lines of spare, modernist design. Gentle fill light softens shadows and makes people look better, which is why it's used traditionally in photography and film.

Illuminating humans – especially faces – presents several specific technical challenges, many of which have been successfully met by fashion photographers and theatrical designers for decades or centuries. The areas where most of the problems lighting people happen are 1) direction and balance; 2) color rendering; and 3) color temperature.

▶ Figure 4.1

The same person lit from different angles: 1. Downlight only, 2. 45° side light, 3. Cross-illumination (Vanity), 4. Even ambient, 5. Even daylight, 6. Harsh side light, 7. Candlelight, 8. Backlit by window. Photos: Randall Whitehead.

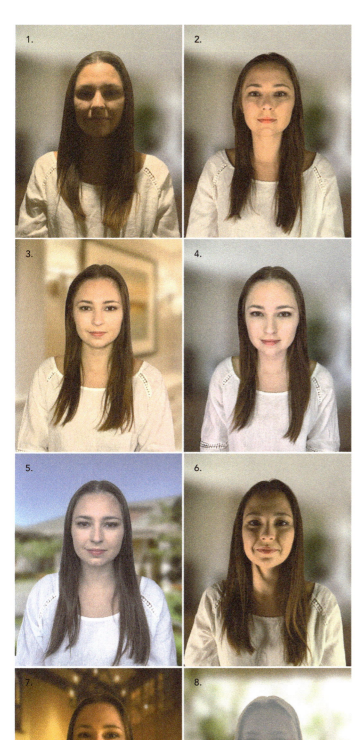

Direction and Balance

The same person can look dramatically different under different lighting conditions. When the face is lit with direct overhead light only, harsh shadows appear under the eyes and in other areas of the face, an unflattering effect at best. In full backlit conditions, unmitigated glare from daylight or other sources can obliterate the face. Ambient light softens the face and makes it much more appealing. Well-executed vanity lighting provides cross-illumination that renders the face at its best for the activities focused on attending to it – doing makeup and shaving. Balancing directional and ambient can shape the face and give it character.

Color Rendering

One of the best reasons to use high color rendering LEDs is that they render the tones of skin, hair, and eyes much more accurately and naturally. In choosing LED light sources, narrow your options. CRI is the only current metric for color rendering you can find, but it's not always accurate. Use your own judgment and test everything before you specify and install.

In Fig. 4.2, which shows shots taken in a specially designed photography studio setup, the women's faces are lit with two different 3000K LED light sources – on the left low color rendering (80 CRI, 80 R9), and on the right high color rendering (95 CRI, 95 R9). In real life we never compare light sources like this, and in this direct side-by-side comparison the low color rendering appears somewhat sickly and greenish. This simply demonstrates that our eyes

◀ Figure 4.2

The effect of high color rendering light sources on skin. On the left the subjects are lit with a 3000K 80 CRI LED, on the right with a 3000K 95 CRI LED. Photos: Russel Abraham, courtesy Soraa.

▼ Figure 4.3

Left: 4000K for daytime use. Middle: 3000K for vanity lighting. Right: 2400–2700K for evening use. Photos: Randall Whitehead.

are very good at detecting subtle but powerful color differences. The dramatic comparison emphasizes what we're really missing with poor color rendering in LEDs. In our experience, we've found that this is still not widely understood, and even the cosmetic industry doesn't recognize it to the extent you might expect, as evidenced by the lighting in a typical department store cosmetic counter.

When lighting people you want everyone to look as good as possible. A subtle rosy glow that suggests a few hours outside in the sun enjoying yourself is flattering to most skin types, and all benefit from optimal color rendering.

Color Temperature

Choose the temperature that's best for the use of the room – if it's used mostly at night, warmer temperatures are better, if during the day, cooler.

CHAPTER 4 Lighting People

Chapter 5

Light Layering

No single light fixture will provide you everything you need to illuminate a room properly. The trick is using a variety of light sources to create a flexible, inviting space. Light performs four basic functions, each with its own light layer. In the layering approach to lighting design, you first identify the purpose of each layer for the different ways the space is used, then blend and balance the layers to create a coherent, comfortable, and inviting space.

Task lighting is lighting by which you do work, such as under cabinet lighting in kitchens, or reading lamps.

Ambient lighting is gentle fill light. It softens shadows on people's faces and fills the volume of a space with a warm glow, as from a roaring fire. Ambient light comes from illumination that is bounced off horizontal surfaces (mainly ceilings, but sometimes countertops and floors) or vertical surfaces, mainly walls. Sources such as opaque wall sconces, torchières, pendant hung indirect fixtures, and cove lighting can be used to create ambient light.

Accent lighting is used to highlight objects and add depth and dimension to an environment. Adjustable recessed luminaires, track lights, portable uplights such as torchières, and directional landscape lights are included in this category.

Decorative lighting adds sparkle to a room. Decorative fixtures are the supermodels of lighting – their main purpose is to look pretty. Chandeliers and candlestick-type wall sconces fall into this category. Decorative luminaires should not be used as workhorses for lighting a room. When they're too bright they can overpower other light layers and design elements.

▶ Figure 5.1

In this room all light layers act in harmony to create a unified experience of beautiful light. Photo: Russell Abraham, Lighting Design: Randall Whitehead, Interior Design: Schippmann Design.

Much of the craft of lighting involves increasing the level of and complexity in a space by focusing on the ambient layer. When gas and then electric lighting were first introduced technologies, the single light in the center of the ceiling of the room was the norm, and many spaces still follow this paradigm even today. As lighting became more sophisticated, designers realized that using the room itself – consciously using reflected light from walls, ceilings, and sometimes floors as an important light source – could transform the space dramatically, making it more inviting and nuanced, setting the stage for a more balanced use of more focused accent and task lighting.

By layering these four functions together you can create environments that welcome visitors while providing usable light for day-to-day activities. Getting a feel for these functions will get you on the right path to understanding how light layering can work for you.

Much of the focus of working with light layering is on the ambient and accent layers, where you're lighting the largest part of a space. In these two layers you're concerned with lighting horizontal surfaces and vertical surfaces, to amplify and soften indirect light from electric sources, but also, in the great tradition of architecture before electric lighting, from daylight. We often like to think of buildings as luminaires – except at a much larger scale.

▶ Figure 5.2

The four light layers:
1. Ambient, 2. Task, 3. Accent, 4. Decorative. Photo: Russell Abraham, Lighting Design: Randall Whitehead, Interior Design: Schippmann Design.

Lighting Horizontal Surfaces

The primary horizontal surface we light is the ceiling, which of course is not always strictly horizontal as in the case with a room with a pitched ceiling. (Other horizontal surfaces that produce some ambient light are floors and work surfaces – although the ambient light here is a byproduct of task or accent light, you can still use it in blending light layers.) Using reflected indirect light from the ceiling as the base ambient layer improves visual comfort, reduces glare, enhances architectural details, and provides the background layer for the other light layers. Illuminating the ceiling draws the eye upward and makes a space feel more open.

There are two basic ways to create the ambient layer with ceiling light: with cove lighting or with mobile uplighting from torchières or directional uplights.

Cove lighting is indirect lighting created by thin linear LED lights recessed inside ceiling coves or soffits. Cove lighting can draw attention to an architectural feature or to conceal lighting fixtures in order to create the cleanest ceiling plane possible. Many manufacturers today offer a wide range of very flexible, small, powerful, and versatile linear LED products that can be used in ways never possible before LEDs.

Lighting Vertical Surfaces

Designers often think in plan view when planning lighting installations. But we experience spaces by orienting ourselves according to vertical surfaces

like walls. Good interior design typically uses a key feature located on a vertical surface like a fireplace or a dramatic piece of art as a focal point to draw you into the space. Lighting vertical surfaces directs attention, provides clear signals for understanding and navigating a space, and enhances visual comfort by reducing contrast between vertical and task surfaces. Artwork, furniture and accoutrements are enlivened, as well as the materials, colors, and textures within the space.

Unfortunately, a quite common default lighting specification, popular with architects, is the use of fixed recessed downlights. Many seem to follow the philosophy that if it's worth doing it's worth overdoing, and recessed downlights are definitely overdone. We call this the Swiss cheese effect. While it's true that a clean ceiling line, uninterrupted by luminaires poking out, can be beautiful and articulate interior volume nicely, direct downlight casts harsh shadows on people, furniture, and art, and fixed downlights can be highly impractical when you decide to move your furniture around. When recessed downlights are required, we greatly prefer adjustable ones as they can be used very effectively in both the ambient and the accent layers.

Wall washing is to walls what cove lighting is to ceilings, and in fact cove and wall washing are often used together to make the best use of interior surfaces for illumination.

Wall grazing is an excellent tool for illuminating vertical surfaces and brings out rich textures by creating contrasting highlights and shadows. This technique can be used indoors or outdoors to draw attention toward an architectural feature, create a dramatic effect, or add interest and a visual focal point that draws the eye into a space.

Linear LEDs today provide a much more effective solution for even lighting of vertical surfaces than directional incandescent sources. Manufacturers offer extruded aluminum channels that can be recessed into the ceiling, tucked behind a drop ceiling detail, or mounted to the surface of the ceiling itself.

▲Figure 5.3

Wall washing with adjustable recessed LED downlights makes this piece of art the focal point of the room and provides part of a beautiful ambient layer. Photo and Lighting Design: Randall Whitehead, Interior Design: Kristi Will Home + Design.

◀Figure 5.4

A reveal is created along the edge of a dropped ceiling to conceal tunable linear LED lighting Photo and Lighting Design: Randall Whitehead.

▶ Figure 5.5

Light layering outdoors. The fine stone work in this garden is dramatically illuminated with wall grazer uplights, carefully concealed to prevent glare. Accent uplights on the plants create another complementary layer, while the fire provides a gentle decorative focal point. Photo and Lighting Design: Randall Whitehead. Photo: Dennis Anderson.

▶ Figure 5.6

Wall grazing with linear LED light accentuates the texture of the brick wall, providing a balance and focal point for this open plan space. Photo and Lighting Design: Randall Whitehead. Interior Design: Kristi Will Design + Home.

▶ Figure 5.7

Linear LED cove lighting provides a gentle warm ambient layer for this bedroom that harmonizes with the horizon line in the magnificent view and makes a good base layer for accent and task lighting, along with future decorative lighting. Photo: Dennis Anderson, Lighting Design: Randall Whitehead.

▲ Figure 5.8

In this room the ambient layer is built through a combination of reflected light from the ceiling luminaire and a hint of subtle undertones reflected off the taupe colored walls. This sets up accent, task and decorative light layers to provide a pleasing balance. Photo: Dennis Anderson, Lighting Design: Randall Whitehead, Interior Design: Turner Martin.

Chapter 6

Light, Color, Materials, Finishes, and Food

It's easy to get mystical about light and color, and many lighting people do, because light is a fascinatingly complex yet strangely elusive phenomena. We never actually see light itself; we only see what reflects it. In our homes what we care most about seeing, besides people of course, is the surfaces and finishes that interior designers, landscape designers, and architects specify: walls, ceilings, floors, furniture, fabrics, paint, plants, water features, and hardscape. And let's not forget other important visual treats like flowers and food. Most of the important surfaces that reflect light are complex natural colors that must be rendered … naturally. No matter how neutral a paint color or texture may appear to be under one light source, it can be greatly affected by the quality of light under different lighting conditions.

One of the qualities of light that must be understood when considering lighting design is "local color" – the specific quality of the daylight in a given geographic location and how it changes over the seasons and in different orientation: north, south, east and west. In the Northern Hemisphere, north light is cooler than south, east, or west light, and winter light in general is cooler than summer light. And light and space are inextricably connected – both daylight and electric light are always affected by the volume, paint color, and structure of a room.

The color of light can alter how rooms and the objects within them are perceived, often significantly. Daylight renders colors "truly," but at night we are used to, and tend to prefer, seeing things under light with warmer color temperatures. Most of us are still very familiar with incandescent light, which tends to be limited to a narrow CCT of 2700–3000K. High color rendering LEDs are widely available in this CCT range as well as cooler and warmer CCTs. Make sure to look at all of your color samples not only under daylight situation but also under the light source you're selecting.

We strongly encourage any design team that includes interior designers, architects, landscape designers, lighting designers, or others to work closely together with light and materials early on in the design process. Given the decisive impact light has on all surfaces, colors, materials, and architectural space, it's essential that the different disciplines collaborate on the creative vision and align on the project requirements and design direction for any project.

▶ Figures 6.1, 6.2

Photos and Lighting Design: Randall Whitehead, Interior Design: Turner Martin.

CHAPTER 6 Light, Color, Materials, Finishes, and Food

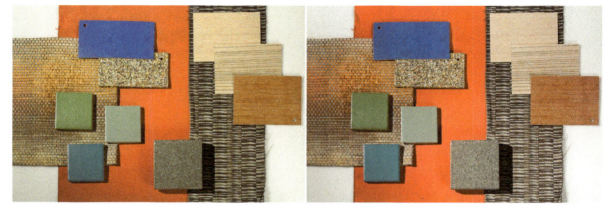

▲ Figure 6.3

Left: Materials under an 80 CRI LED light source. Right: Materials under a 95 CRI LED light source. Photos: Russell Abraham, courtesy of Soraa.

▲ Figure 6.4

Color temperature has an impact on material appearance. All lights sources are 95 CRI, on the left the CCT is 2700K, in the middle 3000K, and on the right 5000K. Photos: Russell Abraham, courtesy of Soraa.

▲ Figure 6.5

Pears and dinnerware under an 80 CRI LED light source (left) and 95 CRI LED light source (right). Photos: Russell Abraham, courtesy of Soraa.

Effects of Color Temperature and Color Rendering

These examples of typical material sample boards used in interior design show the effect of different light sources. These demonstrate by comparison that high color rendering light sources with fuller spectra are preferable, as they bring out the true colors in materials. Even with higher CCT light sources, even as high as 5000K, color rendering has a dramatic effect on how different materials appear and work together. Interior designers and architects have long known that colors and materials shift considerably whether seen under artificial or natural light, so understanding and visualizing how materials, finishes, and rooms appear in both daytime and at night is crucial to a successful design. It's important to show your clients the material boards in both a daylight and evening light situation so that they can experience the color shift, which sometimes can be quite dramatic. Also, light sources with different color temperatures can be mixed in a space, giving depth and complexity to the area.

We do believe in lighting people first, and next the fixtures, furniture, finishes, and accoutrements, but we also believe in lighting food well. Food is not typically thought of as something to light deliberately, but any chef or restaurateur worth their salt knows that lighting is one of the key tools for creating a relaxing ambiance for dining and making food look delectable. Visual appeal is essential to our perception of taste and the enjoyment of what we eat. Colors and textures must be rendered accurately, as we judge many characteristics of food subconsciously and very quickly before we taste it, so if food is not lit properly we won't enjoy it quite as much. We all want to enjoy what we eat as much as possible, and if you cook you know that feeding others well is a driving force in life. Why not make all our meals vibrant and alive with better lighting?

Three Approaches

These projects (Figs 6.6–6.8) show three different ways to work with the interplay of electric light and natural light and its effect on the color, finishes, and materials in the room. In each case the color of local daylight plays a role in the interior and lighting design.

Project 1 uses a monochromatic neutral color for walls, ceilings, and floors to highlight art, while light shapes the space with subtle color variations in light and shadow. The color of the back wall is largely determined by a gentle wash of natural light during the day, and takes on an entirely different character at night, adding dimension and variation to the space. The neutral tones of the walls draw out the richness of the subtle colors and textures of the art.

Project 2 shows a beautiful blend of cooler natural light and warmer ambient LED light, while a full range of color is shown in a counterpoint of the furnishings and surfaces. The rich deep tones of the wood floor and the warm buttery tones of the walls are rendered perfectly by both electric light at night and a carefully calibrated blend of daylight and electric light during the day. The cool harmonizing tones of the furniture set a pleasing contrast to the rest of the room and add coherence with visual clues to the different areas of the open plan room and their functions.

Project 3, a house in a desert climate, projects a palette of light that can be both cool in hot weather and warm in cold weather, and contrasts natural light with warm adobe. The blues of evening light and warm earth tones exemplify one of the classic color combinations found in the indigenous cultures of the Southwest. The direction of the clear desert daylight and the adjustable recessed downlight also play upon the elegant texture of the fabric on the sofa, lending a rich contrast to the smooth adobe walls.

▶ Figure 6.7

Project 2. Photo: Dennis Anderson, Lighting Design: Randall Whitehead, Interior Design: Kristi Will Home + Design.

▲ Figure 6.6

Project 1. Photo: Dennis Anderson, Lighting Design: Randall Whitehead.

▶ Figure 6.8

Project 3. Photo: Eric Zaruda, Lighting Design: Randall Whitehead, Interior Design: Turner Martin.

Chapter 7

Types of Lamps and Luminaires

A vast variety of LED lamps (lightbulbs) and luminaires (fixtures) is available on the market. Here we provide a very general guide to the basic categories of each that you will use in residential lighting.

Lamps with Luminaires vs "Integrated" Luminaires

One of the first things to decide is whether you need a luminaire that has replaceable lamps or is what is referred to as an "integrated" luminaire, meaning that the LED light engine is a fully integrated part of the luminaire. To make it more complicated, many "integrated" LED luminaires also have replaceable "modules," to allow you to switch out the component in the future. There are pros and cons to each approach. We're used to changing light bulbs, but this has always been because they burn out, not because we want to update our house with the latest technology like we upgrade our smart phones. LEDs are marketed as lasting forever, so why would we want to change them anyway? It's all pretty confusing at the moment as we're in a transition phase that will probably last many years. Manufacturers appear to be covering both angles – they are continuing to make luminaires that will accept standard lamp forms, and at the same time innovating new forms of luminaires specifically for LED technology.

Quality of Light First

When choosing lamps or luminaires, always look for the best quality of light first, then consider a range of other criteria, including color temperature, beam spread, mounting options, and compatibility. Look for products made by manufacturers that don't try to make too many products for too many different applications and who instead choose to do a few things well. Because of the rapid growth of new companies in the market, another big issue with picking lighting products is whether a given manufacturer can be expected to last more than a few years. In recent years customers have been left without support for some high-tech products whose manufacturers discontinued products, and this is a perceived risk for the future as technology changes so quickly. You don't want to specify any product that will be obsolete or unsupported in a year or two.

Interior Luminaires

Floor & Table Lamps – These include lamps used on tables or other furniture, torchières, reading lamps, and desk lamps.

Recessed Downlights – Retrofit – These downlights are installed into existing housings and come in three basic types: adjustable, fixed, and wall wash. Retrofit kits are designed to replace existing incandescent or fluorescent downlights with LEDs.

Downlights – New Construction and Remodel – Downlights for new construction are recessed into ceilings and come in three basic types: adjustable, fixed, and wall wash. These are placed between joists before sheetrock is installed.

Downlights for remodel are installed into existing ceilings and come in three basic types: adjustable, fixed, and wall wash. Holes are cut in sheetrock and the downlight housings are installed into them, then wiring is run between or drilled through the joists, above the ceiling line. The wiring can also be run below the joists by cutting slots in the sheetrock, which are then covered with a metal plate in order to meet code.

Track and Rail Systems – These modular systems are usually mounted on ceilings or suspended below the ceilings. They include track, monorail, and cable types.

Wall Lights – Wall luminaires usually provide decorative or task lighting and include sconces and picture lights.

Pendants and Chandeliers – These hang from the ceiling and provide drama and focal points in addition to light. They fall into the decorative category but can sometimes provide useful ambient and task light as well.

Surface Mount Ceiling Lights – Ceiling and flush mount luminaires are extremely practical in areas of high activity such as kitchens, baths, laundry rooms, playrooms, and dens.

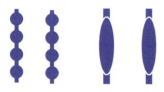

Vanity Lighting – This specialty category of bathroom lighting includes pendants, sconces, bath bars, and illuminated mirrors.

Linear LED Lighting – LED strip and linear type luminaires are extremely versatile, lightweight, and flexible and don't throw off a lot of heat. They are a great source of ambient light as well as low level task lighting.

Exterior Luminaires

Uplights and Accent Lights – These are used in the garden and exterior of the home to accent trees and other plantings as well as architecture. They are sometimes used inside homes as adjustable accent lights on ceilings when there is no depth available for recessed luminaires.

Inground Lights – Inground lights, also known as well lights, are more concealed and lower profile than above-ground lights and are ideally suited for accenting architectural features, facades, or sculptures.

Area Lights – Exterior area luminaires provide general illumination for outdoor areas and can be wall mounted or post mounted.

Path and Step Lights –This category of exterior lighting is focused primarily on safely guiding you and your guests on exterior pathways at night.

Decorative Outdoor Lights – Decorative luminaires used in exterior lighting include pole lanterns, sconces, and pendants. These luminaires are designed to please the eye and provide focal illumination.

Directional Lamps

MR (Multifaceted Reflector) – High color rendering directional LED lamps in the popular MR16 and MR11 formats were some of the first to come on the market for use in residential, hospitality, and retail lighting. They can have a bi-pin base, a GU10 twist-in base, or a screw-in base.

PAR (Parabolic Aluminized Reflector) – These lamps are directional as well but come in larger sizes than the MR16s. They are also available with higher lumen outputs, are made of tempered glass, and can be used outside without a protective covering. Narrow spot, Spot, 16–22 degrees, Narrow flood, 23–32 degrees Flood, 33–45 degrees, Wide flood beam, over 45 degrees.

BR (Bulbed Reflector) – These lamps deliver soft-edged, directional light and can be used for general household luminaires, recessed can lighting, or track lighting. Their lighting is less precise and produces less shadow than PAR bulbs, but they are great for fixtures that use dimmer switches.

Omnidirectional Lamps

A-lamps – These are what we think of as the typical lightbulbs. Manufacturers took longer to develop high color rendering high quality A-type lamps but now many are beginning to come on the market at very good prices.

All illustrations: Clifton Stanley Lemon.

Flame-tip and B-10 – These versatile and popular bulb sizes also took manufacturers a long time to develop, but now many excellent options are available. They are available in standard screw base (Edison Base), intermediate base, and candelabra base.

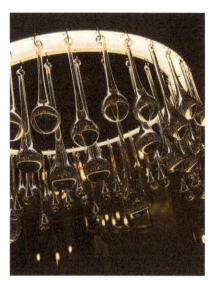

◀ Figure 7.1

This chandelier has integrated linear LED lighting casting illumination down through the crystals. Photo: Randall Whitehead.

◀ Figure 7.2

These antique looking filament lamps are actually LEDs. Photo: Randall Whitehead.

◀ Figure 7.3

LED components are hidden behind a luminous panel at the top of these pendants. Photo: Randall Whitehead.

▶ Figure 7.4

This table lamp from the 1950s is updated with a dimmable screw-in LED A-lamp. Photo: Randall Whitehead.

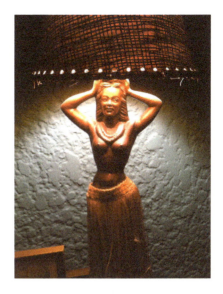

▶ Figure 7.5

Linear LED lighting can come in very flexible ribbons. Photo: Randall Whitehead.

▶ Figure 7.6

Linear LED lighting runs in strips inside these wood pendants to create a wonderful glow. Photo: Randall Whitehead.

Chapter 8

Control Issues

Luminaires are becoming more sophisticated, and so are lighting controls. With LEDs we can now do things with light we never could do before. Even disregarding all the new technology that LEDs have brought to residential lighting in the last decade or so, lighting controls can be difficult for people to understand, operate, program, and adjust.

Having a good overview of the different types of controls systems that are available and what they can do is a good place to start for designers, architects, and contractors to be able to speak more knowledgeably to their clients. Each project is different, based on budget and the needs of the homeowners. Younger customers are sometimes more comfortable with technology, whereas some older clients want something simpler ... but still better than regular switches and dimmers. Smarter systems offer the ability to create scenes instead of just controlling groups of lights.

Basic Needs in Lighting Controls

At the most basic level, there are only two types of control in lighting that we care about in residential application: switching (off and on) and dimming (changing intensity). With LEDs, to these we now add changing color temperature, which is a totally new capability – up until now lamps were only available with fixed color temperatures, and changing color only happened in theater lighting. Most people have no idea what changing color temperature feels like until they see it, and don't yet know if they need it or what they'd do with it.

For the first part of the 20th century, electric light in homes was not dimmed; it was only switched off and on. Dimming for residential incandescent lamps was introduced in the late 1950s and early 1960s by Joel Spira, who went on to found Lutron Electronics. The first LEDs introduced in the late 2000s for commercial use were generally not dimmable. The problem was that luminaires, lamps, power supplies, and controls were mostly all developed by different manufacturers, and components did not work well together. After some pressure from industry and specifier groups, manufacturers gradually improved and standardized the color quality and lumen output of LEDs as well as their compatibility with power supplies and controls.

Even though incandescent is now the old technology, people still want LEDs to behave like incandescents when dimmed – the color temperature gets warmer as the intensity is reduced. Most LEDs today still don't do this. When dimmed they maintain their original color temperature.

If you are using regular dimmable LEDs, get a color temperature that you or your client likes and then just control the intensity. For example, if you are drawn to the color of dimmed incandescent which is 2400K, then specify this color temperature for the lighting. At full capacity it will provide a bright warm light which can also be dimmed down to more intimate level of illumination.

Occupancy and Vacancy Sensors

Occupancy sensors, which turn on lights when people enter a room, are usually used for commercial spaces, but in California, Title 24's lighting code requires that residential bathrooms have switched vacancy sensors. This means that when you enter the room, you must manually switch on the lights, and they will automatically turn off after you have left the room. Dimmable versions of these are available.

Scenes

Beyond regular switching dimmers there are now smart home controls which allow you to turn on groups of light at different levels in order to create different scenes that complement and enhance the settings of a room. Using these successfully means understanding how different light layers work together. For example, in the evening, one setting could be for the ambient lighting to be at 75%, the accent light at 25%, decorative lighting at 35%, and the task light at 15%. You could label this the EVENING setting. Once you are ready for bed you select a few lights to stay on at a very low level to get you and guests safely from the bedrooms to bathrooms and from the kitchen to the bedroom. This could be just the task lights set at 5%, and everything else is turned off. This could be labeled BEDTIME. Some of these dimming systems come with a fade rate that determines the time required to gradually transition from one lighting scene to the next. Typically, these control systems come with four pre-set scenes. This number is important, because no matter how fancy the design of the house or the lighting design, the vast majority of humans have a limited number of "default settings" for domestic life, and typically won't spend the mental energy changing lighting scenes or settings once they've been established. So it's important to work with your clients to get the scenes right from the beginning – more importantly, specify lighting control systems that make it supremely easy for clients to change settings on their own if they are motivated to do so, without having to call tech support or initiate expensive house calls.

Smart Lighting, Smart Home

Some "smarter" lighting control systems connect wirelessly to the lighting through plug-in components while others have a control center which is part of a Whole House system. The more sophisticated systems allow you to control the lighting not only from the wall switches but also from your phone or even from your car. They can also be set to come on at various times a day so that the house will appear to be occupied when you or your clients are on vacation.

With smart home systems, get your clients comfortable with the idea by listening carefully to how they want to use their home environment to fit their lives. These systems can also control the HVAC, security, and sound systems in addition to lighting. You don't want them to be overwhelmed – no one wants a home control system that is smarter than they are. Once it is installed, make sure that you or your clients have a tutorial to familiarize them with this system. In a month, come back and tweak the settings once the clients have gotten used to living in the house.

Every home can be better with lighting control that improves comfort and convenience, enhances security and peace of mind, and saves energy. Today consumers expect technology to be at their fingertips, to make their lives easier, more secure, and more convenient, but new technology solutions often ignore basic human factors like usability and can get in the way of common sense and good design. Manufacturers are gradually beginning to understand this, but have a long way to go to make it easy for homeowners. The important thing is that lighting control systems serve the principles of good lighting design – understanding and balancing layers of light to light people and environments optimally – not the other way around.

▲ Figures 8.1, 8.2

The same room from two different angles and three different lighting scenes. Top: Evening setting, Middle: Bedtime setting, Bottom: Daytime setting. Photo and Lighting Design: Randall Whitehead.

Chapter 9

Designing Sustainably

Since we work in California, our experience with codes for residential lighting is based mostly on California's codes. As of this writing, most U.S. states don't have energy codes as stringent as California's, but may be influenced by California's standards in the future. Even though codes can sometimes seem unnecessary or too complicated, they're not an impediment to good lighting design – LEDs use only 10–20% of the energy of incandescents. And as we show throughout this book, their quality is as good if not better than incandescents, which is mostly what they have replaced in residential use.

▶ Figure 9.1

Welcome to the world of efficient, beautiful light.
Photo: Randall Whitehead.

Impact of Energy Codes for Lighting

Codes and regulations, in combination with the highly energy efficient technology of LEDs, have resulted in an unprecedented reduction in lighting energy use – from a 1978 baseline, almost a 90% overall reduction. This has been accomplished largely while maintaining or improving the overall quality of lighting products. Energy codes have resulted in stimulating and directing innovation in LEDs and provide direction to the market. Healthy, safe, high quality LEDs are now widely available.

Why It's Important

Now lighting energy use is a much smaller part of total energy use, but it has one unique characteristic – it's the most visible use of energy. And where LEDs have led in public awareness of energy efficiency we now need to follow with other appliances in the home, such as electrifying stoves and water heaters. Successfully meeting the challenges of climate change starts in the home, where we can control our energy use and carbon emissions.

Basic Requirements

It's very difficult to summarize California's energy codes for lighting in one paragraph, but they basically require:

- High efficacy light sources (≥45lm/W)
- High CRI light sources (>90 with R9 >50)

- Light sources with CCT of ≤4000K
- Light sources dimmable to 10%
- Light sources with lifetime of 15,000 hours and lumen maintenance of 25,000 hours
- Dimming and occupancy sensors in specific locations like kitchens and bathrooms.

These requirements are the current code as of this writing, the 2019 Title 24 standards, for remodel or new construction, which is mostly what you'll be doing as a lighting designer. There are many more detailed requirements, and each state has its own energy code. We provide resources for California code information in the Bibliography. If you're not sure how to meet code on your project, work with your electrician, home energy consultant, and local building authorities. You can also visit the California Energy Commission website for more detailed information.

Efficiency is Beautiful

Choose lighting first for beauty, health, functional reasons, then meet code. Understanding energy code requirements in residential lighting (even if you're not always strictly required to meet certain efficiency standards) will allow you to design with both energy efficiency and high quality of light in mind. For the informed designer these are entirely compatible goals.

Chapter 10

The Design Process

Play Well with Others

A successful home design is a result of a collaboration. Depending on the size and scope of a remodel or new construction the design team on a project can include an interior designer, an architect, a lighting designer, a landscape architect/designer, and a contractor. The clients are part of the team as well, but they are really the bosses. Our job as designers is to come up with ideas and solutions that meet the needs of clients ... and to make sure that design, construction, and installation run as smoothly as possible.

This can't happen when team members are working independently without communicating – everyone needs to stay in the loop. Even though what might seem to be a relatively benign change can affect other aspects of the design. For example, if the contractor decides to flip a door swing and doesn't let the other professionals know it can cause costly revisions down the road. If the lighting designer is not informed, it may result in the controls for the room behind the open door and require moving the switching to the other side. It also may mean that a particular piece of furniture or art selected by the interior designer may not fit on a wall because the open door is taking up wall space. This would require the return of the selected piece and time involved finding a smaller substitute.

In reality there will always be issues during the design and installation process. It is much better to work with the other team members to come up with a solution that can be presented to the client, instead of just saying there is a problem. If you are supportive of your fellow professionals, they will remember that and recommend you for other projects. These newly forged work relationships can last for years or decades, providing a steady source of new jobs.

Gather Information

Your first task as lighting designer is to gather as much information as possible on the project. Floor plans alone are not enough – you need elevations and sections as well. They tell you how tall the walls are and whether the ceiling is flat or sloped. You also need reflected ceiling plans which indicate things like beams, coffers, skylights, soffits, heating and ventilation vents, and sprinkler heads. All of these will have a significant impact on where luminaires can be located and how power will be routed to them.

It's impossible to do a successful lighting design without a furniture plan – you cannot light an empty space effectively. For example, if you are trying to lay out lighting in a dining room, your initial inclination might be to locate a chandelier or a pendant luminaire in the center of the room. If the interior designer has located a sideboard or console on one wall, that could move the dining room table off center, and the decorative luminaire would then be located in the wrong spot. The interior designer may say that they haven't picked out the specific pieces, but they will be working from a furniture layout in order to know what pieces to look for. That's what you need. It will determine the correct position for hanging fixtures and floor plug locations.

Testing Ideas – Renderings and Mockups

Perhaps more than other design fields, lighting design depends heavily on trying ideas out in real life, with mockups, samples, and renderings of ideas. It takes some skill and imagination to apply lighting effects on top of design sketches, as light doesn't follow hard lines, plus it's not easy to draw or render in reverse – where you usually start with a blank white canvas and add darker lines, shapes, and shadings, with rendering lighting you must start with dark and add light. Fortunately there are many design tools available today like Photoshop, and most architects can produce sophisticated renderings fairly easily. And by all means learn how to draw well with pencil on paper, or use paints, pastels, or ink. This skill will serve you well in any design field, and lighting is no exception. Experiment with starting on black paper and adding light.

Make sure to review the kitchen countertops and backsplash material selection submittals. Highly polished surfaces will reflect the under-cabinet lighting like a mirror, creating distracting pools of glare that can ruin the effect of comfortable task lighting in the kitchen. A material with a honed or matte finish that will defuse the light is preferable. Check if the overhead cabinets in the kitchen have a recess at the bottom where under-cabinet lighting can be hidden. If the cabinets are Euro-style without a reveal at the bottom, a continuous run of linear LED can be installed in an aluminum extrusion.

Also review the material submittals for the finish on hardware like doorknobs and draw pulls. The metal components of the decorative luminaires should complement these architectural details. They don't have to match but should be in the same family – chrome, brushed chrome, nickel, brushed nickel, silver, zinc, and pewter will all work together. The same goes for gold, brass, antique brass, bronze, and copper.

All the top lighting professionals do mockups of lighting effects, test lamps and luminaires under different conditions, and have entire rooms devoted to samples of equipment to use to try out new ideas and experiment. Most lighting people are constantly experimenting and judging light primarily by how they see and experience it in real life. Bring this practice of direct testing and experimentation to your craft of lighting design and you will be much more successful.

Class is in Session

If you're working with a couple, it is really helpful is set up meetings where they both can attend. This saves you having to say everything twice and it is much easier to come to mutual decisions. Use your time wisely.

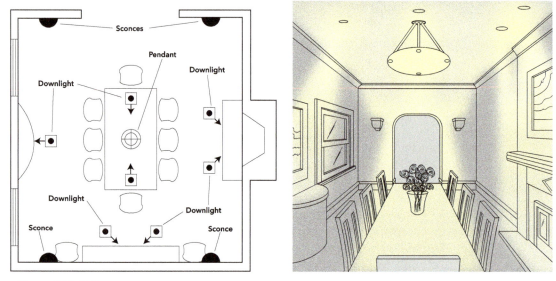

▲ Figures 10.1, 10.2

Translating a plan view (left) into a rendering that conveys the experience of the room, even if it's a rough approximation, helps both the clients and the entire design team visualize the impact of lighting decisions. Illustration: Clifton Stanley Lemon.

Even impromptu sketches can help convey lighting ideas well. Sometimes the rougher they are the better – they can be done quickly, show ideas in a human way that makes clients more comfortable, and don't look as final as detailed realistic digital renderings. On the other hand, when you can manage it, realistic digital renderings of proposed lighting schemes are sometimes also easy to do if suitable photographs or architects' renderings are available to use as a base layer. If you can take advantage of more sophisticated software tools, by all means do so, and use them to amplify your creative freedom, not to replace it. You still have to understand light layers and good design principles no matter how you choose to visualize your lighting design concepts.

▶ Figures 10.3–10.6

This series of renderings demonstrates different techniques of modeling design concepts to convey the spatial and aesthetic experience of the spaces. Renderings and Lighting Design: Lux Populi.

CHAPTER 10 The Design Process 67

Chapter 11

Typical Lighting Fails

In the last generation or so, North Americans have seen a dramatic improvement in the overall quality of residential interior design in terms of the level of finishes, use of sophisticated equipment like European appliances and cabinet systems, and of course new LED luminaires. Yet for all the money spent on fancy granite countertops or built-in refrigerators, more often than not lighting is poorly conceived and executed. It's an afterthought. Bad lighting can ruin a good interior design, or at least make it less successful than it would have been with a better understanding of the basics of good lighting design. To learn what to look for in good lighting design, we find it quite valuable to look at what makes bad lighting design, especially when it may not be immediately apparent to an untrained eye dazzled by shiny Euro-flash design details.

Ubiquitous lighting fails fall into several categories:

- Missing or unbalanced light layers
- Poor luminaire placement
- Incorrect light levels
- Glare
- Poor color temperature
- Poor distribution
- Poor luminaire selection.

Typically we see several types of fails in one installation. Then there are those situations where so many things are wrong with the lighting that nothing short of major surgery will provide a remedy. But as a design professional, you should proceed as a doctor presented with a patient with multiple ailments would – first, do no harm, then identify the problems and their causes, addressing one at a time with the goal of healing the patient holistically.

Wrong in So Many Ways

If one image could serve as an example of what NOT to do with LED lighting, this would be it. The color scheme of the room is pleasing, there

▲Figure 11.1

Photo: Serghei Starus/ Depositphotos.com.

are beautiful flowers, nice comfortable furniture, expensive cabinetry – this wasn't done on a shoestring budget. But all the intended design effects are badly compromised by the lighting. We see poor luminaire selection and placement, incorrect light levels, poor light layer management, glare, inconsistent light color, and above all poor color temperature. Light this cold, probably in the range of 5000K, is suitable for hospital operating rooms or industrial manufacturing environments, but not for homes. The blinding icy palette overwhelms everything. The lack of modulation and differentiation in the light layers produces the kind of flat ambience that people hate in office buildings lit with high CCT fluorescent troffers. In the kitchen, highly reflective surfaces produce irritating spots of glare reflecting off poorly located fixed downlights, and the under-cabinet lights glare in your eyes as you sit on the sofa. To save this room, you should first change every luminaire to warmer color temperatures in all the luminaires and specify LEDs with better color consistency. Next, changing and relocating all the downlights so that they illuminate walls and don't produce glare from the ceiling will help. The interesting circular flush mounted ceiling luminaires are not appropriate in this room – adding something to break up the flat open lines of the space, like pendants or torchières will provide more relief for the eyes.

▲ Figure 11.2

Photo: Katarzyna Białasiewicz/Depositphotos.com.

Euro-Posing

When you first see this photo you think "what a clean beautiful modern Euro kitchen!" right? And it is that, but it's compromised by bad lighting. Because the surfaces are all so light colored there is a nice amount of ambient light. But poor light layer management creates an uneven impression, and poor luminaire selection and placement cause distracting glare. The under-cabinet spot downlights create inelegant scalloped beam patterns on the backsplash and spectral effects on the shiny countertops. Diffuse, unobtrusive linear LEDs would be a much better choice here. Also, the fixed recessed downlights are very poorly placed – insulting the cabinets with uneven smears of light, and certainly casting harsh shadows on any people in the kitchen. A better approach would have been to take advantage of the light-colored surfaces and bounce ambient light off the walls by using wall wash downlights or uplight/downlight sconces. Indirect lighting could also be placed on top of the cabinets which are mounted above the pass-through area.

Specular Reflections

The problem here is glare. This extremely common problem is illustrated by a close-up shot of a highly polished granite countertop that produces distracting bright spots of reflected light from the LED under-cabinet lights above it. People dearly love their granite countertops (nothing says status like granite in the kitchen!) but frequently fail to realize the implications of lighting them like this. The first and best solution to this is not completely a lighting solution – work with the interior designer to specify countertops with buff, matte, leather, or flame finishes that will disperse bright directional lights and make the environment much more pleasing visually. Next, use soft, diffused linear LED undercounter lights.

▲ Figure 11.3

Photo: Randall Whitehead.

CHAPTER 11 Typical Lighting Fails

The Tragedy of the Single Bulb

A single glary bulb in the ceiling is pretty much the opposite of the entire idea of lighting design, yet it remains a very common approach in many homes. Far too often, people simply just don't think about lighting and opt for a "simple" solution. In this gloomy room, there are no light layers, no differentiation, nothing to draw you in. The glaring luminaire casts unwholesome shadows everywhere in a greenish tint. Another problem is that the luminaire is a fan light, which might seem convenient until you get tired of the huge distracting shadows of the fan blades dancing around the ceiling.

▲Figure 11.4

Photo: Randall Whitehead.

▲ Figures 11.5, 11.6

Photos: Randall Whitehead.

The Eternal Swiss Cheese Ceiling

Here the problems are poor light layer management and poor luminaire selection and placement. The ubiquitous grid of fixed recessed downlights in an open plan space – or any space for that matter – is not good lighting design. The illumination in these situations feels flat, and the areas have no sense of separation or intimacy. Fixed recessed downlights also cast harsh shadows and don't create the ambient layer in a room as they're basically lighting the floor and other horizontal surfaces. Many top lighting designers globally avoid recessed downlights completely, but if you must use them, used adjustable ones so that you can illuminate walls and make a beautiful ambient layer.

▲ Figure 11.7

Photo: Alexey Zarodov/Depositphotos.com.

Warm, Dramatic, Expensive, and Not Quite There Yet

In a room with all light-colored surfaces like this one, you don't need much light to fill the room with an ambient layer. The stone finishes on the walls and floor create a beautiful warm feeling for the room, but the main problems here are glare, shadows, poor light layer articulation, and lack of appropriate vanity lighting. Remedies? Use adjustable recessed downlights aimed at the walls to create the ambient layer; remove the downlights over the sink that cast shadows on the face, and add soft warm vanity lighting at either side of the mirror. Then perhaps add a small decorative luminaire somewhere – or even just a candle – to delight the eye and put things into proportion.

▲ Figure 11.8

Photo: Dennis Anderson.

The Drama Queen Entry

This installation exemplifies very poor light layer management, opting for an overly contrasting approach to lighting this entry. The intent is more to impress guests with your exquisite taste in art rather than to welcome them into your home, but the effect falls flat. You could fix this room by keeping the dramatic light on the sculpture and possibly adding cross lighting to articulate its shape more effectively, a very effective strategy for sculpture. Then add an ambient layer by throwing some light on the ceiling, possibly with sconces or linear lights. Then gently light the walls with adjustable recessed downlights. You could show off your fabulous art *and* make guests feel comfortable right away– that would make a much better impression, don't you think?

▲Figure 11.9

Photo: Marko Poplasen/Depositphotos.com.

Poor CCT and Lack of Focus

This room gets credit for having a cove lighting detail. The light source is well hidden, and the illumination is very even. Unfortunately, color temperature is too cool for a residential setting and the CRI is too low which gives the lighting a greenish cast. The large diameter recessed fixtures just create scallops of light on the wall. A linear recessed LED wall grazer would have done a better job. Two or three really cool modern pendants, installed in the center line of the ceiling, could have added some real architectural jewelry. The first one would be centered over the dining room table, and then the additional one or two luminaires could be spaced equidistantly. The back wall display case in the dining room area would benefit from some linear lighting installed in each of the squares, mounted along the front face of the casework.

Part II | Interior Lighting

Overview

The purpose of this part of the book is to address the home room by room and lay out guidelines to lighting them optimally. This section includes case studies of rooms which will detail the design concepts, along with the types of luminaires and lamps used. Color temperature and color rendering metrics will also be noted so that you become familiar with how rooms look under different lighting conditions. With enough practice, you'll be able to accurately judge color temperature and color rendering of light in real homes just by looking at it.

At the heart of good lighting design is how it makes people feel in the space. Do they feel welcomed in? Is the lighting complementary? Does the lighting illuminate the architecture and the objects within the space successfully? Are there controls organized and located for ease of use? We can call this "human centric" lighting, but that term means something rather different to most of the lighting industry. For us the most important things to light in the home are not things at all, but people.

Lighting plays different roles in different rooms. Some rooms are multi-functional and need more light options. Other rooms are more limited in their use and may not need all four light layers. An entry may rely more heavily on decorative and accent sources and much less on ambient and task lighting. Kitchens often serve as gathering places for the family in addition to food preparation, so here more light options are needed.

As we mentioned in Chapter 1, the modern Western concept of the home as a collection of single purpose room still prevails, but as culture, demographics, and climate change, this idea is evolving into something different and more flexible. Grown children are living at home more and more, families are evolving in new directions, and open plan living is immensely popular now. This involves the kitchen being open to the living room and dining room areas, and the entry and family room/media room are becoming integrated into the open plan concept. The challenge is to create a sense of separate spaces within this open plan concept, and to make sure that the lighting subtly imparts a sense of connection while articulating each separate use area.

We will convince you that the default grid of recessed downlights is not good lighting design but its antithesis, and that you can spend a lot of good money on bad lighting and detract from a beautiful interior design. With the tools you will learn here you'll be able to approach home lighting thoughtfully and holistically.

▶ Figure INT.1

Lighting Design: Randall Whitehead.

Chapter 12

Kitchens

Kitchens used to be separated from the rest of the house by doors or pass-through walkways between the kitchen and dining room. Because the kitchen was a separate space, the lighting didn't necessarily need to integrate with the other spaces. Today the kitchen is open to the rest of the entertaining areas and seen from the family room, dining room, great room, and even the entry, so kitchen lighting needs to reflect this use pattern and blend in.

Modern kitchens typically feature a centrally located island used as a food preparation surface. Decorative luminaires hung above the island create a visual separation without interrupting the flow of the space. The trends in kitchen design here are to use two or three pendants spaced out equidistantly, single oversized ones with a linear shape, or clusters hung at various heights with an asymmetrical design.

▶ Figure 12.1

Photo: Misha Bruk.

Blend Without Bending

You need a balance of all layers in the kitchen and connected spaces. Pendant luminaires over the island provide decorative and task layers. The ambient layer can be introduced by adding linear LED lighting on top of the cabinets to create an inviting glow of illumination on the ceiling to help soften shadows and to integrate the ceiling plane into the overall architecture. The accent light layer can be provided by interior illumination for glassed face cabinets or display niches. Or adjustable recessed downlights can highlight a feature such as a flower arrangement in the center of the island when it's not being used for food preparation.

The main light layer in the kitchen of course is the task layer. An excellent strategy for this is linear LED strip lighting mounted below the overhead cabinets (hidden behind a fascia) at the front edge of the cabinets to illuminate countertops. This approach gives a consistent, even wash of light and is far superior to a series of puck lights, which can create distracting scallops of light along the backsplash.

High gloss countertops such as polished granite can be very difficult to illuminate since they are a specular surface with a mirror-like finish that will reflect whatever light source is installed. Luckily, the trend is toward the use of more matte surfaces for the countertops, including honed, flamed, or leather finishes for granite, composite stone with matte surfaces, along with

soapstone and marble slabs. The challenge for this under-cabinet lighting is to keep them from being seen when people are at a sitting position in the other areas of the open plan layout. We recommend placing the LED strip in an extruded aluminum channel, to direct the light toward the backsplash at a 45° angle.

Consider installing a recessed linear LED in the ceiling, installed parallel to the front face of the cabinetry. This will project an even wash of illumination onto the face of the cabinets, as well as provide illumination inside the cabinets when the doors are opened up.

▶ Figure 12.2

Photo: Eric Zaruba, Interior and Lighting Design: Turner Martin.

Color Me Comfortable

The last element to consider is the color (Kelvin temperature) of the light, along with the color quality (atmosphere) of the light. The kitchen needs to look like it is visually integrated into the other spaces. It's important to have all the lighting of a consistent color temperature throughout all the rooms.

Now there is warm-dim technology that allows LED lighting to appear warmer in color when dimmed. We think this is great, but it can tend to be on the pricey side, especially when it needs specialized controls. A more cost-effective solution would be to choose dimmable LED sources for all the rooms that are part of the open plan, specified with the same color temperature.

Designers are now tending to gravitate toward color temperatures as low as 2400K. An incandescent bulb normally has a CCT of 2700K, and when dimmed goes down to 2400K. With the lower CCT LED, you're simply starting with the color temperature you would have ended up with anyway. Then the brightness can be raised or lowered depending on whether you're doing food prep or in the entertaining part of the evening. For some people 2700K is more comfortable, and it doesn't shift the colors in the room too much.

Even if you do choose 2700K, it is still going to be considerably warmer than daylight. One of the mistakes that people make is selecting all of their finishes, including paint colors, fabrics, and tile, in a daylight situation. Review all these samples under the color of light you select for evening, to see what they will look like in a nighttime setting. Under these warmer color temperatures pewter starts to look like brass, red looks orange, and white looks yellow. Since half your time is spent in the house after dark, you want to make sure that these color shifts are comfortable.

Some people like a cooler color temperature for food preparation. This is where a tunable linear LED source would be a good idea. You can dial in a color temperature anywhere from 5000K down to 2250K – basically going from daylight to candlelight.

The last element to think about is the CRI (color rendering index). Be sure to select something that has a CRI of 90 or higher. There is a lot of product out there that's in the 70–85 CRI range; generally it's just not good enough. These LED products last a long time; you don't want to be stuck with something for 17 years that doesn't feel quite right. It's like being caught in a bad relationship from which you can't escape.

Kitchen Project 1

This kitchen is designed in a transitional style – it's traditional but has some very modern elements to it. It's a fun design direction to work with but comes with a few challenges.

This project shows a wonderful balance of lighting layers and is especially enhanced by the exterior lighting, which extends the visual field of the room and by showing the garden gives us a subliminal reminder of where our food comes from. You don't normally think of the garden as part of interior design, until landscape lighting comes into play. Then you can see why it makes sense to think of your house and garden as a whole space rather than a collection of rooms and outdoor spaces. Highlighting the garden brings the outside inside at night, extending the feeling of space and eliminating the "black mirror" effect of windows at night.

The 2400K LED under-cabinet lights provide beautiful warm task lighting that provides a nice glow and doesn't show distracting reflections on the matte surface of the countertop.

Two drum pendants use 2700K dimmable LED A-lamps and provide task light for the island. They add visual focus for the kitchen and warm ambient light.

▲ Figure 12.3

Photo: Dennis Anderson, Lighting Design: Randall Whitehead.

Kitchen Project 2

This well-planned kitchen in a contemporary style shows a beautiful blend of elements and light layering. The uplights on top of the cabinets define the shapes in the interior architecture and provide the ambient layer, and the even under-cabinet lighting and the downlights on the window wall are all successfully integrated. The lightly colored cabinet surfaces and walls help provide a soft ambient layer, and the warm color of the wood floors also brings the ambient light color to a pleasing balance.

    It's important to remember that no project, or home, is perfect forever. This project is an example of beautiful interior design and great lighting design, and it shows things that could have been done better in retrospect and might be addressed in the next remodel. For instance, the recessed downlights illuminate the counter, sink, and window wall nicely but would benefit from repositioning – they're too close to the molding, which catches distracting scallops of light. And the beautiful blown glass pendants provide a soft illumination and real decorative focal point above the kitchen island but would more effective if they were used in a cluster or were larger in scale.

▲ Figure 12.4

Photo: Dennis Anderson, Lighting Design: Randall Whitehead. Interior Design: Kristi Will Home + Design.

Kitchen Project 3

This project, located in Phoenix, Arizona, with its dark colors and clean lines, is not a typical example of "desert design." The lighting follows the vision of the interior designer, which was to create a space that was harmonious with the client's lifestyle. We love the art in the space and the sense of light and shadow. It's kind of moody, but what's wrong with that? The dark colors speak to a cool respite from the desert sun. Additional task lights can be turned up to increase the light levels, but having something that's a bit more dramatic than a typical kitchen is unexpected and wonderful.

This pendant's rectangular shape follows the shape of the table it's illuminating. The luminaire is lamped with screw-in 2700K high color rendering, dimmable LED A-lamps to give us that wonderful glow. While this is primarily a decorative luminaire, the A-lamps also give us some ambient uplight that bounces off the ceiling. This luminaire is used to create a sense of a space within a space – the dining area – and to draw people in with a welcoming glow.

The recessed downlights are adjustable rather than fixed, which illuminates vertical surfaces rather than casting harsh shadows on people's faces with light from directly above, a disadvantage to the typical way in which downlights are used. Adjustable downlights give flexibility and allow light to be directed to tabletops, art, food, or anything in the space that needs highlighting. This flexibility comes in handy when furniture is moved around in the space.

Soft, non-glaring under-cabinet lighting works in conjunction with a mirror to give a visual focal point and to expand the sense of space in the room.

▲ Figure 12.5

Lighting Design: Randall Whitehead, Interior design: Turner Martin, Photo: Jeff Zaruba.

Kitchen Project 4

▶ Figure 12.6

Lighting design: Randall Whitehead, Interior design: Bethe Cohen Design Associates, Photo: © Douglas A. Salin.

All four light layers – task, accent, ambient and decorative– are nicely balanced in the design of this spacious kitchen. Kitchens are natural gathering places for families and casual entertaining, and kitchen lighting should be able to adapt to the function at hand. Warm-dim linear LED provides a robust and flexible ambient layer that accommodates the prevalent dark and reflective surfaces and softens the task lighting.

This design required a soffit to house heating, ventilation and cooling systems (HVAC). This provided an opportunity to integrate ambient LED lighting architecturally. Careful early coordination with the architect and interior designers helped this integration to be executed successfully. Linear LED cove lighting is housed in the soffit in a triangular aluminum extrusion with a frosted lens which projects light out at a 45° angle so that it spreads and diffuses evenly over the ceiling. The linear LED ceiling soffit is warm-dim, ranging from 4000K down to 2200K. This range of color temperatures adds flexibility to the space throughout the day and evening.

Two pendant lights provide an additional layer of indirect uplighting in the ceiling so that the center of the ceiling does not fall into darkness. These luminaires also provide filtered downlighting as task light for the kitchen island and the breakfast bar. They have a brushed nickel finish that pairs nicely with the faucet, stainless steel sink, and the drawer pulls. When specifying luminaires, consider that metal finishes don't necessarily have to match all the other hardware in the room, but they should be in the same family.

The European-style cabinets against the back wall came with their own task lighting in the form of puck lights (so called because they are round and shallow like a hockey puck). These are not an optimal lighting choice as they provide visible uneven arcs of illumination – linear LED under-cabinet lighting here would have been a much better choice. This would provide evenly distributed illumination on the work surface, avoiding the hotspots of light you see on the blue tile back splash.

Additional LED linear lighting is installed on the underside of the breakfast counter. This keeps the space below the countertop where the stools slide in from being a dark void. It also takes some of the visual weight away from the countertop itself. A channel, routed out on the underside of the countertop, houses the linear LED and hides it from view.

▲ **Figures 12.7, 12.8**

This galley kitchen uses low key task and accent lighting to create an inviting space that blends seamlessly into the living room and dining room areas at either end. Linear task lighting provides illumination for the countertops while a suspended track system highlights art. Photos: Randall Whitehead, Lighting and interior design: Turner Martin.

▲Figure 12.9
This realistic rendering shows clients visualize how specific styles and sizes of pendants would look over their kitchen island. Lighting Design: Randall Whitehead.

▲Figure 12.10
This large kitchen benefits from abundant ambient and task lighting. LED linear lighting is installed above and below the upper cabinets. Photo: Robert Whitworth, Lighting Design: Randall Whitehead, Kitchen Design: Kristi Will Home + Design.

Chapter 13

Bathrooms

The bathroom is where our fundamental design principle of lighting people first is most applicable. Well-designed lighting in the bathroom should be a top priority. Yet more often than not people just accept whatever the builder has installed. How many times have we seen a photograph of a vanity with the recessed downlight directly over the sink? It might make for a great dramatic shot – of the interior designer's work – but try to imagine yourself standing at the mirror with that harsh light hitting the top of your head. Remember when, as a child, you would hold a flashlight under your chin to create a scary face? With single-source downlight illumination the same thing happens, only in reverse: long dark shadows appear under your eyes, nose, and chin. This is extremely bad lighting for trying to apply makeup or shaving. Who wants to look at a scary face first thing in the morning, especially if that face is yours? Refer to Chapter 4 for an example of the deleterious effects on humans of direct downlight-only illumination.

There are also countless bathrooms across the country with only a single surface-mounted luminaire above the mirror, a situation that is only slightly better than a single recessed downlight. At best this illuminates the top half of the face, letting the bottom half fall into shadow. It's especially difficult to shave in this lighting situation – there are only so many ways you can tilt your head to catch the light.

For the best vanity task lighting, install two sconces flanking the mirror area above the sink to provide the necessary cross-illumination. Look for luminaires that are translucent and dimmable. The center of the luminaire should be mounted at eye level, about 5'6" above the floor. If you're living with a person who is much taller or much shorter than you it's a good idea to choose a luminaire that is long enough to give everyone a fair chance of getting good lighting. Dimmable LED vanity luminaires are widely available.

When specifying light sources for the bathroom, color temperature, color rendering, and lumen output are all particularly important. Knowing what each of these three qualities of light means in application is essential for successful bathroom lighting. (See Chapter 3 for more details.) Lamp and luminaire manufacturers have gradually begun to include detailed information on all these specifications on product packaging, but it is not consistent.

▶ **Figure 13.1**

Photo and Lighting Design: Randall Whitehead.

Lighting for Tubs and Showers

▶ Figure 13.2

Photo and Lighting Design: Randall Whitehead.

While the task area at the vanity is the most important to illuminate correctly, the other areas of the bath bear careful consideration. Tubs and showers need a good general light. For this purpose, recessed luminaires with diffusers are commonly used and relatively effective. Using a recessed adjustable luminaire rated for wet location allows some flexibility as to where the light is directed. As designers and homeowners like to specify wonderful, interesting tile, elaborate plumbing luminaires, and even niches for art, they can install directional luminaires to highlight these exciting elements. There are many LED recessed luminaires now on the market that are rated for wet locations.

Ambient Lighting

Indirect lighting in a bathroom adds a warm overall glow to the space. Cove lighting that directs light upward can provide gentle ambient ceiling illumination, and linear LED is a good choice for this application as it has a very small footprint, high flexibility, and is available in dimmable versions. In the bathroom, we recommend using a warmer color temperature – between 2700K and 2400K. 2700K is the color of incandescent light at full brightness; 2400K is the color of dimmed incandescent. For bathrooms with higher ceilings, pendant or close-to-ceiling luminaires can also be used very effectively for ambient ceiling illumination.

Accent Lighting

Ambient illumination in the bathroom sets the stage for accent lighting, which highlights plants and art pieces. When homeowners are entertaining, the room most frequently visited by their guests will likely be the powder room. This space can be treated differently from the other bathrooms. No serious tasks are going to be performed by guests here – it's a place where people will wash their hands or check their hair and makeup before rejoining the party.

At the vanity lights should be just a flattering glow. A pair of translucent vanity lights on either side of the mirror with a luminaire in the middle of the ceiling will do the trick. Some powder rooms do double duty as guest baths for overnight houseguests. If this is the case light the bath as you would a master bath, also making sure to put the various lights on dimmers to allow for flexible control over the illumination levels.

Bathrooms Project 1

▶ Figure 13.3

Photo and Lighting: Randall Whitehead, Interior Design: Kristi Will Design.

This guest bath has a clean, fresh, and luxurious look. A pair of sconces flank the mirror above the sink, providing cross-illumination for the face. The center luminaire in the ceiling adds an overall glow of illumination to the room, providing both ambient and decorative layers to the design.

Installation details for vanity lights are important. The light source should ideally be at eye level. When creating drawings, note that the junction boxes for the sconces should be at 5' 6" above the finished floor. If the shade material is not in the center of the luminaire, then the junction box mounting height needs to be adjusted. This particular pair of wall sconces has the shade mounted at the top of the luminaire, instead of in the center or running along the entire length of the luminaire. The mounting hardware is centered in the back plate, so in order for the shade to be mounted at 5' 6" above the finished floor call out for the mounting height of the junction box needed to be lowered by 4 inches. It's always best to specify your luminaires before the electrical rough-in so that the correct mounting heights of the junction boxes can be determined in advance.

For vanity light levels, look for light sources that produce between 1100 and 1600 lumens. Color temperature and CRI are also important considerations. A cooler CCT may render the colors of white walls and tile work more accurately but will be less flattering to skin tones. Always use light sources with the best color rendering for vanity light (no lower than 90 CRI) as skin color is of paramount importance here. Luminaires or lamps with warm-dim capability will allow for cooler colors during the day and warmer colors at night but must also maintain high color rendering.

Don't be afraid of using overscale luminaires in small spaces. This ceiling luminaire is 24" in diameter, for a bathroom that is 9 feet by 5 feet. It hangs down slightly from the ceiling to provide an ambient glow of light to spread across the ceiling, while the patterned diffuser adds a soft spread of illumination and strong decorative visual interest.

Bathrooms Project 2

▶ Figure 13.4

Photo and Interior Design: Wright Simpkins, Lighting Design: Randall Whitehead.

This high-end master bath uses both natural light and LED lighting to full advantage in a beautifully balanced design. Three frosted glass sections create a partition between the master bath and the master bedroom which allow natural light to flow into the bath from the adjoining room during the day. The panels were incorporated into the design as a way of getting natural light into the master bath which had no exterior windows. Mounted along the perimeter of each glass section is a run of LED linear lighting providing illumination after the sun has set. The LED linear luminaires use dimmable, RGBW color tunable LEDs, which can provide a full array of colors including rich warm whites. They amplify the illumination from the pendants, providing an additional layer of lighting for people's faces, and double as backlighting for a decorative screen mounted to the panels on the master bedroom side of the wall.

The two mirrors centered over the sinks use pendant luminaires instead of wall mounted vanity lights. These are fitted with frosted oblong lamps. The shades hang with centers at 5'6" above the finished floor. While these are beautiful and ornate, they still provide excellent cross-illumination at the mirrors for applying makeup or shaving. The two sinks are spaced out so that they share the center pendant, instead of having to use a pair of pendants for each of the two sinks. They use screw-in dimmable 2700K, 90 CRI LED A-lamps.

A tasseled center ceiling pendant fixture provides additional architectural bling.

Bathrooms Project 3

▶ Figures 13.5, 13.6

Photos: Blake Marvin,
Lighting Design: Techlinea,
Architect: Geddes Ulinskas.

In this bathroom lighting is fully integrated with the architecture. On this project the lighting designer worked with the architect who wanted the wall surrounding the floating vanities to provide illumination for the room by using 360 Möthe translucent drinking glass tumblers. These also provide a very even facial illumination at the mirrors for shaving or applying makeup.

A local solar panel company was hired to fabricate this wall of light. Dimmable linear 0.5W, 2700K, 93 CRI LEDs were positioned on a panel at 4" on center, which accommodated the mounting of the 3-1/2" glass tumblers with a 3/4" spacing. This panel included blank spaces for mounting the mirrors, vanity, and plumbing. Transformers for the LEDs are mounted under the vanity for easy access.

A single pendant fixture hangs between the two mirrors (we see its reflection in the shower door). Additional lighting for the room is provided by a recessed LED downlight rated for wet location, installed in the ceiling area above the shower. This recessed luminaire has a 16W LED, and the pendant fixture is an 11W LED, both with a 90 CRI.

Bathrooms Project 4

This master bath pulls out all the stops, but in a subtle, minimalist way. The interior and lighting designer collaborated closely to create two custom-fabricated illuminated mirrors that float above the vanity. They provide even lighting for the face with dimmable, color tunable LEDs.

Concave oval dishes with a brushed stainless steel finish were faced with ovals of frosted Starfire glass (leaded glass with no greenish tint). The mirrored ovals were silvered in the center, leaving a frosted glass frame to provide illumination. The fabricator needed to create the metal forms deep enough to allow a 2-1/4" setback to prevent diode spotting and to allow light to bounce off of the polished reflective curved interior surface out through the frosted lens framing. Output at full brilliance was calculated at 1200 lumens. In order to keep the profile as small as possible the power supplies were installed in the ceiling, next to an access hatch.

The walk-in shower has an architectural reveal (a linear slot) that runs above the ceiling line and accentuates the rectangular shape of the tile. A run of wet location rated linear LED lighting, housed in the reveal, is mounted in a U-shaped lensed channel. This concentrates the beam spread to 10°, allowing an even wash of illumination down the back wall without significant light loss at the base. A pair of wet location rated recessed luminaires, centered in the ceiling, are available for additional light if needed.

▶ Figures 13.7, 13.8

Photos: Michelle Drewes,
Lighting Design: Techlinea,
Interior Design: Pamela Pennington.

▲ Figure 13.10

Bathrooms can be quiet retreats, filled with art and art objects. Subtle lighting helps create this spa-like feel. Consider using warmer colored LEDs, somewhere in the range between 2700K and 2400K. Photo: Dennis Anderson, Lighting Design: Randall Whitehead, Interior design: Turner Martin Design.

◄Figure 13.9

The ideal illumination at the sink is a pair of luminaires mounted on either side of the mirror. Look for 2500–300K lumens, 2700K and 95 CRI. Photo: Misha Bruk.

▼Figure 13.11

A dropped ceiling creates a linear trough which runs along the perimeter of this powder room. A linear LED washes the lines down rules with gentle illumination. The small mirror at the sink has an opaque wall sconce mounted above to provide some illumination for guests. Photo: Dennis Anderson, Lighting Design: Randall Whitehead.

Chapter 14

Living Rooms

Is your living room a natural gathering place? Or is it the space that people pass by on their way to the media room or the kitchen (where the food and drinks are)? In the home of decades past, the living room was only used when guests arrived. This "living" room was essentially a kind of surreal museum diorama separated by an invisible braided rope that kept the kids out until allowed entry only on special occasions and of course on their best behavior. Most of the time, its fancy furniture and appointments were kept unused, mostly for show, in the service of maintaining status. To work successfully with people in designing their ideal homes means understanding the powerful emotional drivers behind gaining and maintaining status. In humans (as well as many other species) status can take precedence over food, water, territory, sex, or other elements essential to life. The drive for status also explains many seemingly irrational design decisions.

Today many living spaces are now open plan rooms that connected to each other rather than distinct rooms separated by walls. The kitchen, living room, and dining room are often part of one large area. The living room areas within these open plan spaces are being used more, so we should make them comfortable and inviting and a part of daily life, where the real "living" happens.

▶ Figure 14.1

Photo: Dennis Anderson, Interior Design and Lighting: Joseph Hettinger.

Oh the Humanity!

Living rooms with high ceilings, or any rooms for that matter, can be a gift … or a major pain. How do you make a voluminous room feel inviting? If you install accent lighting – either track, mono points or recessed downlights – who will be the brave person that gets up on that tall, tall ladder to relamp and adjust the lights? Good lighting design addresses these issues.

High ceilings can be intimidating and make people feel insignificant in the space – the same feeling of humility you get when you enter a house of worship with vaulted ceilings. This is appropriate for a church, temple, or mosque, but not how you want to make your family and guests feel in your home. It's better to subtly draw people into a space with an elemental feeling like the glow of a crackling fire. This comes from the addition of *ambient* light, an indirect lighting source which is bounced off the ceiling and then back into the room. You can hide the light source using crown molding, an architectural cantilever, or box beams. This soft fill light helps

physically and emotionally to warm up a space. However, ambient lighting by itself is not enough. It creates what is referred to as the "cloudy day effect," where everything in the room has the same visual value.

You need to add the other three light layers to create good lighting design: *decorative*, *accent*, and *task*. Depending on the size of the room, hanging one to three pendant fixtures can create a secondary ceiling line, which gives a more human scale to the space. If these luminaries have translucent elements they can be both decorative and ambient light sources at the same time. Reading lights would fall into the category of task lighting. Having little pools of illumination in the seating areas helps draw people into the space and enhance comfort.

▶ Figure 14.2

Photo and Lighting Design: Randall Whitehead, Interior Design: Kristi Will Home+ Design.

Uplight and Out of Sight

A main key to successful lighting design is the addition of ambient light. It softens the shadows on people's faces and helps create an inviting environment that welcomes people into the room. As we mentioned above, there are real and faux architectural solutions to this challenge. In more traditional homes you can have a crown molding running the perimeter of the room with indirect lighting concealed behind. For more modern homes it can be a shelf-like cantilever that hides the linear light source.

Using a linear LED product provides you with a solution providing long life and low energy consumption. You can choose your color temperature to match incandescent light at full brightness (2700K) or dimmed incandescent light (2400K). You can also choose an RGBW LED source that gives you a full range of colors, including realistic gradations of an incandescent feeling illumination. You can also specify an LED that goes from 5000K (daylight) down to 2150K (candlelight).

Another faux architectural solution is to install a series of box beams. These are non-loadbearing hollow beams, which also act as decorative elements. They should be 2 feet to 6 feet down from down from the ceiling, depending on the height of the room. Indirect lighting can then be installed on top of these beams to provide the very desirable fill light. The same beams could also hold recessed adjustable fixtures that would be installed into the bottom side of the beam making them more accessible for relamping and adjusting.

A quick and non-architectural solution would be to add torchère lamps, as the source of ambient light. Select a style that has an opaque or semi-translucent shade. You don't want to draw attention to the light source. You can also use portable uplights, hidden behind tall potted plants to cast a shadow pattern up along the ceiling. Using any one of these options is a step in the right direction to create a room that says, "Hey, come in, sit down, relax, enjoy."

Living Rooms Project 1

▶ Figure 14.3

Photo: Dennis Anderson, Lighting Design: Randall Whitehead.

This very modern residence was built around the owner's art collection. The challenge was to create something that was inviting to family and guests while also highlighting the paintings and sculpture.

The design team decided to add unique luminaires with a decidedly sculptural feel. This layered paper pendant fixture was designed by Ingo Maurer. Over three feet in diameter, it provides both decorative lighting and ambient light for the room, and is intriguing without being visually overwhelming. Above the light source, a blue lens projects a discreet azure glow onto the ceiling, and an opening at the bottom projects a shadow pattern onto the floor.

This is an example of a design that uses the decorative layer expertly, as the pendants keep the eye moving within the room and into the next, forming a natural visual connection in the space. They're not too bright to dominate, even though the ambient light levels are relatively low.

Adjustable recessed luminaires with square trims that play off the angular lines of the house highlight the art and tabletops, providing the accent layer. They also light the walls, providing a subtle ambient layer. These luminaires present the best use of downlights, as they are unobtrusive, directed correctly, and draw the eye to the objects being lit rather than to the light sources. They are lamped with dimmable LED MR16s that have a color temperature of 2700K and a CRI of 90.

From this room you get a glimpse of the library which features another sculptural pendant. These two luminaries don't have to match, they just have to relate.

Living Rooms Project 2

▶ Figure 14.4

(After) Photo: Jeff Zaruba, Lighting Design: Randall Whitehead, Interior Design: Turner Martin Design.

This living room in this Scottsdale, Arizona home uses light to create an alluring retreat. The challenge with this project was finding a way to create accent light for the space. The home is well insulated against the harsh temperatures of the desert. Because of the beamed ceiling construction, using recessed luminaires was not an option, so a series of track runs were installed on the ceiling in between the beams. The system uses low voltage LED MR16 lamps to gently highlight art and tabletops. Each luminaire is fitted with a louver to help hide the light source.

    A pair of over-scaled Balinese wall sconces are installed on either side of the fireplace. Their long curved arms let them float out into the space, adding a lot of dimensionality. They each use a screw-based LED 2400K T-lamp which helps to illuminate the entire shade evenly. Two other sconces flank the picture window on the right. They are designed to project light onto the wall, creating an illuminated proscenium for the spectacular view outside.

    The floor lamps have both a top diffuser and a bottom diffuser so that the light source is shielded from view, whether people are standing or seated. The right-angle arm of the lamps allows the shade to cantilever out over the seating area, offering an unobtrusive reading light. A dimmer is built into the switch so that the light level can be raised or lowered depending on the task at hand. Two dimmable screw-in LED A-lamps with a color temperature of 2400K and a CRI of 90 were used in each of the luminaires.

    Just after dusk, the landscape lighting comes on, accenting the patio area with its sculptural cacti and the giant boulders beyond. This keeps the windows from becoming black mirrors at night, where you end up seeing your own reflection in the glass instead of the view of the exterior.

    This shows how the space looked like before the remodel. Along with the lighting, see how changing the windows, flooring and fireplace façade really changed the look and feel of this room.

▶ Figure 14.5

(Before) Photo: Randall Whitehead.

Living Rooms Project 3

▶ Figure 14.6

Photo: Dennis Anderson, Lighting Design: Randall Whitehead.

The 12' ceilings in this living room make it hard for the room to feel intimate. A solution was to use four large pendant lanterns, which fulfill several different functions in the space. The lanterns, designed by Ingo Maurer, are more than 3 feet in diameter. This might seem huge, but it turns out to be just the right size for the room. They drop down 36 inches from the 12' ceiling plane, creating a secondary ceiling line which adds some human scale to the space. They provide a decorative element as well as a good amount of diffuse ambient illumination. Each lantern has five light sources, four which are located near the top, aimed horizontally, and one which is aimed down through the bottom aperture.

Square aperture adjustable recessed downlights illuminate the coffee table, sculpture, and the burnished metal fireplace façade. They use 12V MR16 lamps with a variety of beam spreads, from tight spots to wide floods, and have a color temperature of 2700K and a CRI of 90.

Two tabletop reading lights have flexible arms which allow people to direct the light where they need it. Floor plugs were integrated into the initial lighting design to eliminate visible cords and tripping hazards.

When evening falls we see how the room takes on a warm inviting glow. Screw-in LED lamps with a color temperature of 2400K were used because they have the quality of dimmed incandescent. The small aperture adjustable recessed downlights have an aiming angle of 45° and a rotation of 358° and can be pointed in any direction.

▶ Figure 14.7, 14.8

Photos: Dennis Anderson, Lighting Design: Randall Whitehead.

Looking back toward the rest of the main floor of this home we notice a band of vertical light intersecting the thick divider wall. This is part of the overall lighting design concept, and adds a great amount of visual interest to what otherwise might be a mundane architectural detail. A recessed inset, painted in a matte white finish, was created on either side of the opening to hide a run of linear LED lighting, which is dimmable and has a color temperature of 2400K and a CRI of 90. It makes a great night light.

Living Rooms Project 4

▶ Figure 14.9, 14.10

Photos: Misha Bruk, Lighting Design: Randall Whitehead, Interior Design: Turner Martin Design.

A successful lighting design keeps the eyes moving around the room. When a living room is illuminated with a single light source, which is often the case, all focus naturally goes to the singular luminaire, the brightest thing in the field of vision. When light is layered it shapes the environment subtly but powerfully. In this living room illumination comes from many sources and falls onto many surfaces.

The accent lighting comes from adjustable recessed downlights which use 12V MR16 LED lamps with a color temperature of 2700K and a CRI of 90. They highlight the wall art, the objects on the tabletops, and the wooden sculpture. One of them is directed toward the wooden screen on the right. Some of the downlighting hits the textured black and white rug and the green-stained floor.

There are two decorative luminaires seen in this shot. On the left is a metal and resin Balinese wall sconce. It uses a 4.5 W screw-based LED T-lamp with a color temperature of 2400K and a CRI of 90. The floor lamp uses two of the same bulb. It has an opaque metal shade with a translucent shade overlay which keeps the floor lamp from drawing attention away from the other objects in the space. The top of the shade has a translucent diffuser which gives a wash of ambient light up toward the ceiling and back into the room.

The accent lights are slightly cooler in color in order to the render the hues of the objects more accurately. The decorative fixtures use a warmer color temperature so that even at full brightness, they have the look of dimmed incandescent light sources.

On the left side of the living room, three floating shelves have been installed. Along the front edge of each of the shelves there is a run of LED linear lighting which is housed in a triangular aluminum extrusion, painted black. Light is directed back toward the collection of photographs at a 45° angle, which reduces reflection on the glass frames.

A large horizontal mirror mounted above the black lacquer chest reflects daylight back into the room from the row of sliding glass doors on the opposite wall and also make this living room feel larger.

The lighting is controlled by a mid-range dimming system which has been divided into switching groups. The adjustable recessed downlights directed toward the walls are on one dimmer; recessed downlights that project light downward are on their own separate control; wall sconces (there are three in the space) are dimmed independently; and the portable luminaires are plugged into dimmed receptacles. These independent dimmed groups can then be blended together to create different "scenes," providing a range of light levels that adapt to how the room is used at different times of day or night.

▲ Figure 14.11

The lighting in this living room sets the tone for a relaxing mood by balancing a very warm ambient layer with bright points of decorative LED pendants and chandelier bulbs. Photo: Dennis Anderson, Lighting Design: Randall Whitehead.

▲Figure 14.12

All light layers contribute to a dramatic yet relaxed effect here, with some interesting visual surprises. Photo: Dennis Anderson, Lighting Design: Randall Whitehead. Interior Design: Turner Martin Design.

Chapter 15

Dining Rooms

What Faith Popcorn called the "cocooning effect" in the 1980s seems to be having a strong recurrence in the time of the Covid-19 pandemic, except that as of this writing people are hunkering down in their own homes instead of going out to restaurants with friends by necessity, or law, rather than as a trend of choice. In the 1980s and 1990s people were using the kitchen island as the space for casual entertaining and serving food, a trend that still holds today, but the dining room has been enjoying a new renaissance.

Dining tables designed for flexibility are popular, for instance folding down to allow for intimate seating for four or expanding to seat more diners. Even homeowners who have kept their large tables sometimes choose to push them against a wall for occasional buffet dining. These changes require a more flexible approach to lighting in the dining room, beginning with rethinking the chandelier.

▶ Figure 15.1

Photo and Lighting Design: Randall Whitehead, Interior Design: Turner Martin.

Rethinking Chandeliers

For eons the dining room table has been centered under the chandelier. Many people have spent countless hours of their lives making sure that this alignment was just perfect. As dining room tables began to become a little more flexible in their positioning, the chandelier in the center of the space started getting in the way. For homeowners who want a traditional feel, but with the flexibility to create a more flexible room layout, there are a number of good choices:

1. Choose a decorative luminaire that hangs closer to the ceiling so it doesn't look odd when the table doesn't happen to be in the center of the room.
2. Select a pendant light on a pulley system that allows you to raise or lower the luminaire. There are many European-inspired LED pendants available, primarily in contemporary styles.
3. Hang a traditional multi-armed chandelier of metal and crystal in a recessed dome or coffer so its visual relationship is linked to the ceiling configuration rather than the table location. In a remodel project where this option is prohibitively expensive or there is inadequate attic space for a dome, a decorative ceiling medallion, rosette, box beams or painted pattern can create a similar illusion.

Size and Positioning

When choosing the size of a decorative luminaire for your dining room table, you need to consider not only the table but also the specific proportions of your dining room. For sizing, a good rule of thumb is to add the length and width of the room together, and convert the number from feet to inches. For example, if the dimensions are 12' x 14', then look for a luminaire that is around 26" in diameter. It's better to go a little bit larger than a little bit smaller, so consider specifying a 30" diameter luminaire over a 24".

When determining hanging height, the bottom of the luminaire should be 30" to 36" above the table surface. If your ceiling is higher than the average 8', raise the luminaire 3" more for each extra vertical foot of ceiling height. These are just guidelines for creating a good proportion of objects in space and can vary depending on the layout of the room or if the ceiling slopes. Allow time for on-site adjustment. Chandeliers normally come with additional lengths of chain or cable. Many people living in modern style homes are using multiple pendant-type luminaires instead of just one. It ultimately comes down to an aesthetic call.

Both traditional chandeliers and modern pendants should be used in combination with adjustable recessed downlights to provide accent illumination for the table. A decorative luminaire cannot be the only source of illumination. A middle accent light, located in between a pair of decorative luminaires, could highlight a flower arrangement in the center of the table. Two adjustable recessed downlights, located on either side of the luminaire, could be used to cross-illuminate the tabletop. This would add sparkle to the dishes, silverware and even the crystals in a more traditional chandelier.

Make sure the two outside downlights are not pointed straight down. This will cast harsh shadows on the people at both ends of the table and could create glare from a reflective tabletop, such as one of glass, lacquer, or highly polished wood. Keep them pointed at an angle from the vertical that is less than 45 degrees, so light will hit the tabletop first, giving a soft complimentary under-lighting of people's faces. At 45 degrees or more, the light may glare into people's eyes. The downlights can be redirected toward the wall when the table is being used for a buffet.

A large chandelier may require additional support at the junction box. Most standard junction boxes will support luminaires of up to 50lbs. Check with the manufacturer to find the weight so the electrical contractor can accommodate a heavy chandelier with more support. Large or ornate chandeliers installed in high ceiling areas may benefit from a pulley mechanism that is mounted above the ceiling to lower the chandelier for ease of changing bulbs and cleaning.

The Ambient Layer

Whatever solution you choose for lighting the dining table, this alone will not complete the lighting scenario. Ambient light and additional accent lighting should still be considered. While decorative luminaires will provide some illumination for the entire dining room, they can easily overpower the rest of the elements in the space if turned up too brightly.

Adding ambient lighting is relatively straightforward. Most of the options work well: torchières (floor lamps that project light onto the ceiling); opaque or semi-translucent wall sconces; and cove lighting. If the dining room you are working on has a dome detail, the perimeter can be illuminated with low profile LED cove lighting so that fill light is bounced off the dome's interior. If it is a pitched ceiling with trusses that are parallel to the floor, LED linear lighting can be installed hidden on top of them to provide ambient illumination. Non-structural box beams can also be installed to hide indirect lighting.

The Accent Layer

Two or three adjustable recessed downlights located over the dining room table already address accent light for the table itself and the centerpiece. Sometimes single downlights that provide accent light for centerpieces are integrated into chandeliers. The next spaces to consider as areas in need of accent light are the walls, the side table or buffet, and plants.

For art on the walls, don't feel that every piece has to be illuminated. It's all right to let some pieces fall into secondary importance. It lets them be "discovered" as guests take a second look around the room. Add one or two adjustable recessed downlights to accent a side table, buffet, or console. A silver tea service will sparkle and a buffet dinner will look even more scrumptious when highlighted this way.

Plants can be uplit, downlit, or both. Broad-leaf plants like fiddle-leaf figs are better lit from above or backlighted. Smaller leafed plants like ficuses can be lit from the front, casting leaf patterns on the walls and floor. They can also be uplit, which creates a shadow pattern on the walls and ceiling. Palms are best shown off when they are lighted both from the top and from below. The sculptural quality of a cactus calls for lighting from the front at a 45-degree angle and preferably off to one side in order to add dimension.

Candles Count

Candles should be used correctly as well. Typically at the dinner table you artfully place candlesticks flanking the centerpiece. When you and your guests sit down at the table that candle flame is right at eye level. When you look at the flame for a while then cast your gaze toward the guests, you'll notice that there is a "black hole" where their heads used to be, like the effect you experience after someone has taken a flash picture of you. To solve this problem, use candles that are either lower or higher than eye level. That way you'll get that soft golden glow, but the candle will not distract when looking at the person across the table. Also, realistic flicker flame LED candles are available in many shapes and sizes, and several can be controlled with a handheld remote.

Controls

Dimmers offer many levels of illumination in the dining room. To show off the decorative chandelier when entertaining, bring the level of illumination down to a glow allowing the entire luminaire to be seen, without glare. The wall sconces and accent lights should also be dimmed to create a balanced illumination, enhancing the other elements of the dining room. When you want to use the table to play a board game or do paperwork or it is time to clean up, you can bring the level of light in the luminaires up to full brightness. These controls can simply be dimmers which are designed to work seamlessly with LED sources, and a reasonably priced wireless system would be the next step in an upgrade. Or these controls can be part of a smart house system, which would have keypads on the wall in addition to the ability to dim lights through an app.

The Bottom Line

Light layering in the dining room, as in the rest of the house, is the key to good lighting design. By blending different sources of light together, you will be able to create an overall feeling of comfort and drama. This allows the chandelier, pendant luminaires, and sconces to become the architectural jewelry for your home … especially in the dining room.

▶ Figure 15.2

Photo and Lighting Design, Randall Whitehead, Interior Design: Michael Merrill.

Dining Rooms Project 1

This dining room has an 18' ceiling spanning two stories. A main design challenge in this project was how to make the space feel more intimate. Part of the solution was to add a cluster of pendant fixtures over the dining room table instead of a traditional chandelier. These were dropped down to a height of between 36" and 48" above the tabletop. Staggering the heights can be more visually interesting than having them all uniformly hung. These pendants are fitted with frosted, dimmable screw-in LED filament bulbs. These have the look of old Edison bulbs, are available in a wide variety of shapes, and can be mixed to add more visual interest. Each bulb has a light output of 450 lumens with a CRI of 90.

    Sconces were installed on either side of the fireplace above the mantel, mounted at 6' 6" inches above the finished floor. This also helps to add a human scale to the room. They are the same sconces that are used on the second story open hallway, which helps tie the two areas together. The sconces have woven shades that fit tightly enough against the wall so that the light source cannot be seen from below. They use dimmable LED A-lamps which have a color temperature of 2700K and a CRI of 90.

    Adjustable recessed low voltage LED downlights have been installed to illuminate the art. Because the ceiling is so high, the ones used to highlight the paintings in the dining room are positioned close to the second story railing in order to facilitate relamping and redirecting beam spreads.

▲ Figures 15.3, 15.4

Photo: Ken Will, Lighting Design: Randall Whitehead, Interior Design: Kristi Will Design.

Dining Rooms Project 2

▶ Figure 15.5

Photo: © Douglas A. Salin, Lighting Design: Randall Whitehead, Interior Design: Bethe Cohen Associates.

This dining room is all about drama. The red chairs make a bold statement, while the cluster of chandeliers adds the icing to the cake. With a dining room this big, a single chandelier, in the right scale, might feel overpowering. The use of three smaller chandeliers is a creative solution. The round shape of the luminaires, along with their cascade of bubbles, plays off the curvilinear layers on the ceiling.

Adjustable recessed low voltage downlights wash the gossamer curtains with illumination and light up the flowers in the center of the table and the objects on the trestle table located below the mirror. Each of these uses a 120V 11.5W LED MR16. These bulbs are available in a warm-dim version so that they feel incandescent as they are lowered in intensity. In between three of the decorative fixtures is a single recessed downlight that lights the center of the table. It also uses a 120V LED MR16.

The recessed fixtures have a round aperture to complement the curvature of the room. These are recessed adjustable fixtures that use a 120V LED MR16 bulb with warm-dim capabilities, matching those in the decorative fixtures.

Dining Rooms Project 3

In this newly remodeled home, many of the original 1940s details have been preserved. The interiors have been modernized, but not ultra-modern – this is often referred to as "transitional" interior design. What is so good about LED light sources now is that they can be easily integrated into homes that are more traditional. High quality, widely available LEDs can match and exceed the light quality of traditional incandescent and halogen light sources while offering superior energy performance and much longer lifetime, and LEDs are much more adaptable and flexible and can fit into traditional luminaire and lamp forms.

All four light layers are well balanced in this dining room. Often luminaires can perform double duty, adding two layers at once. For instance, the pendant luminaire and the wall sconces provide both decorative and ambient light layers. They have translucent diffusers at the base of the shades to hide the light sources from direct view, and to bounce light up toward the ceiling.

Accent lighting comes from adjustable recessed downlights that use GU10 base MR16 LED lamps. These are line voltage (120V) luminaires that don't require transformers, reducing installation costs and eliminating one component that could fail. Two recessed downlights that cross-illuminate the bowl of bromeliads on the table are set at a 35° angle so that they wash the tabletop with illumination but don't glare into people's eyes. These luminaires, along with the ones that illuminate the wall, have a color temperature of 2700K and a CRI of 90. The decorative luminaires use 2400K lamps with a CRI of 90 in order to add additional warmth into the space.

A view of the dining room from the kitchen shows how lighting connects the two rooms while also creating a subtle sense of separation. This is a subtle and sophisticated way to delineate space and function in homes without necessarily using architecture or furniture.

A good rule of thumb for the hanging height of a pendant luminaire or chandelier over a dining room table is to install it so that the bottom of the luminaire is 36" above the tabletop. This can vary, based on the shape of the luminaire and whether multiple luminaires have been clustered together.

This is one example of why it's so important for the architect, interior designer, lighting designer, landscaper, and contractor to work as a team. This gives the client a much more cohesive design and results in fewer issues during construction and installation.

▲Figures 15.6, 15.7

Photos: Dennis Anderson, Lighting Design: Randall Whitehead.

▼Figure 15.8

Photo: Dennis Anderson, Lighting Design: Randall Whitehead.

Dining Rooms Project 4

▶ Figure 15.9, 15.10

Photos and Lighting Design: Randall Whitehead, Interior Design: Turner Martin Design.

Done in an elegant, eclectic modern design style that might be called Asian Fusion, with deep chocolate colored walls that highlight art and decorative luminaires, this dining room shares an open space with the living room and is separated by a freestanding fireplace. Three 2-foot-wide soffits hide newly installed plumbing and ventilation systems while adding interesting architectural detail to what was previously a plain flat ceiling and providing enough depth for recessed downlights.

Adjustable recessed downlights wash the tabletop with illumination and highlight art and art objects. As some of these downlights were already installed before this remodel, new ones matching the originals were added. The preexisting luminaires used 12V halogen MR16 lamps. All downlights were relamped using 2700K, 95 CRI LED MR16s. This reduced the energy use from 50W per luminaire down to 11W. The trims for the recessed luminaires in the soffits were sprayed with a highly heat-resistant brown paint to match the soffits.

The interesting pendant over the table is made from two components, a 5" diameter striped glass pendant and an inverted metal stool suspended around it. This unexpected combination creates a one-of-a-kind luminaire at a reasonable cost.

A different view of the dining room shows some of the other elements of the room. One of the three soffits along the wall houses recessed downlights and a wire-way for the pendant luminaire. A built-in console featuring sliding shoji panels offers a warm glow of illumination. The shoji panels are backlit with a continuous run of LED linear light mounted along the front edge of the console, installed with the LEDs pointing down so that they rake the back side of the shoji screens with light. With a color temperature of 2200K and a CRI of 93, this is the warmest light in the space. The shelving inside the console is held back 3 inches from the face so that the light can go all the way down to the base of the console. This allows the linear lighting to provide a second function, illuminating the interior shelves where glassware, dishes, and linens are stored.

The turned wood sculpture in the corner provides a focal point for the room. This is illuminated from the front by an adjustable recessed downlight and is backlit with a small uplight included to add dimensionality to the piece. The 2700K color temperature and the 95 CRI enhance the warm tones of the sculpture and the other wood elements in the room.

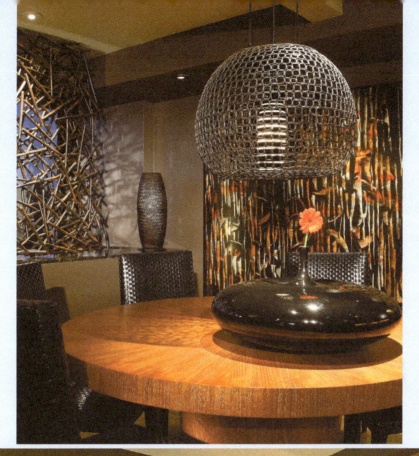

▲ Figure 15.11

This impressive chandelier provides a decorative element and a source of fill light, along with the wall sconces. All luminaires use LED lamps with a color temperature of 2700K and a CRI of 95. Photo & Lighting Design: Randall Whitehead, Interior Design: Kristi Will Design.

▼ Figure 15.12

A linear LED pendant draws guests to the table but doesn't compete with the clean modern architecture. A series of sconces provide fill light for the space, while adjustable downlights illuminate the walls and stacked niches. All the light sources are 2700K with a CRI of 90. Photo: Dennis Anderson, Lighting Design: Randall Whitehead, Interior Design: Nicki West.

▲ Figures 15.13, ▼15.14

In this dining room, hollow beams house adjustable recessed LED downlights. The beams float down from the ceiling so that linear LED lighting could provide fill light for the room. LED picture lights were mounted above the two paintings. The 2200K color temperature matches the color of the candlelight on the table. Photos: Douglas Sandberg, Lighting Design: Randall Whitehead, Interior Design: Michael Merrill Design Studio.

Chapter 16

Bedrooms

Bedrooms unfortunately usually get the least attention when it comes to lighting. Architects or contractors typically don't have a good game plan for lighting the bedroom. We often see a fan in the center of the room and four recessed downlights in each of the corners, along with a couple of bedside lamps, a solution that epitomizes lazy lighting thinking. Bedrooms have four primary functions: sleeping, sex, reading in bed, and packing for trips, and obviously lighting impacts all of these. (A television in the bedroom negates three of these functions.)

▶ Figure 16.1

Photo and Lighting Design: Randall Whitehead, Interior Design: Turner Martin Design.

We will emphasize, yet again, how important it is to be seen in a flattering light. Consider the idea that lighting you and other living beings in your home is more important than lighting the stuff you want to show off. Looking good typically starts with the addition of ambient light to the default single-source directional or decorative light. Dimmers can go a long way toward making the bedroom feel more alluring. The rule of thumb is: "the darker the room, the better you look." And as we all know … it's not about how you feel, it's about how you look, so look as fabulous as you can at all times!

Ambient illumination makes all the difference. Use cove lighting, with linear LED strip lighting hidden in a simple cantilever or crown molding, running around the perimeter of the bedroom. Pick one color temperature, between 2700K and 2200K, that flatters skin tones, or choose a full color changing version so that you can dial in other colors, such as pink, peach, amber, or twilight blue. If you do select a color changing version, make sure that it also includes white LEDs so that you can get realistic gradations of incandescent colors. This means selecting something that is RGBW, not just RGB, which doesn't offer the subtle gradations needed. Also, choose the highest color rendering rating you can find, at a minimum above 90 CRI.

Indirect LED lighting can also be mounted on the tops of canopy beds, armoires, and bookcases – LED linear strips are small, easily hidden, and can fit in places where you may not have thought of using light before. A less architectural but entirely effective way of providing the ambient light layer is to use floor lamps or wall sconces that project light up toward the ceiling.

Task lighting at the bedside for reading is essential. Although many people are reading on mobile devices such as pads or phones which project light, ambient light makes it easier to read on these screens. And other activities undertaken in bed such as knitting, beadwork, Sudoku, crossword puzzles, or even eating also require task light.

The optimum task light comes between your head and your work surface. Anything above your head, like a recessed downlight, will cast the shadow of your head onto your work surface. When locating task light near the bed, place yourself in the bed in the position you typically read, then mark the spot just above your shoulder as the location for the junction box.

Some options for task lighting at the bed include wall-mounted swing arm or "pin-up" plug-in luminaires and tabletop bedside lamps with flexible arms. Sometimes the headboard can get in the way of positioning the light correctly, so take this into account when choosing luminaires.

In a long rectangular room a ceiling-mounted luminaire in the center of the ceiling, or a series of them, can make the room feel more welcoming. With high ceilings, hanging luminaires will help humanize the scale of the room, adding a bit of architectural bling to the ceiling line. These are primarily decorative fixtures, but they often provide a secondary ambient light layer.

▶ Figure 16.2

Photo and Lighting Design: Randall Whitehead, Interior Design: Turner Martin Design.

Closets

Many of us start our day in the dark and must choose an outfit for the day. Later in the day, we may realize that we have two different colored socks on or the blazer or skirt that we thought was black turns out to be navy. Natural daylight is perfect for identifying colors, but unfortunately unavailable before sunrise. If we try to select our outfits under the wrong light, color can shift significantly – reds look orange, whites look yellow, and it's nearly impossible to tell the difference between black, navy blue, and charcoal gray under low CCT light (2700K or below). One practical tip for closets is to use color tunable lighting, or at least two light sources with different color temperatures – one closer to daylight (4000K to 5000K) and one closer to warmer light preferred in the evening (2700K or warmer). A light source that is close to the color of the environment you're dressing for will help you choose the right clothes and look (and therefore feel) better … and we will take this opportunity to remind you yet again that lighting is all about how you and other people look.

Remember, you spend half your life in the bedroom – why not feel attractive while you're in there?

Bedrooms Project 1

▶ Figure 16.3

Photo: Dennis Anderson, Lighting Design: Randall Whitehead.

This guest bedroom is warm and inviting, a result of a thoughtful balance of interior design and lighting. It's best when interior designers, architects, contractors, and lighting designers can work together as a team; it helps projects to be more cohesive and always leads to better design.

A pair of recessed adjustable luminaires mounted above the bed illuminate the painting and the wall behind the bed. These are low voltage luminaires using LED MR16 bulbs. Line voltage (120V) versions of MR16s and other small form lamps are now readily available. Line voltage light sources eliminate the need for transformers, reducing both luminaire and installation costs. The recessed luminaire on the right illuminates the left side of the painting, and the one on the left is doing the opposite – this technique is called cross-illumination. Cross-illumination provides a better wash of accent light than if luminaires were pointed directly at the art, and also helps to eliminate glare by directing light away from the viewing angle.

The shelving is subtly illuminated using linear LED lighting, installed on the underside of the shelf and mounted flush with the front edge. A painted-out wood facia hides the light source which is installed in a triangular extrusion with a frosted lens, aimed at the back wall of the casework. Linear LED lighting is superior to the puck lights we often see in finished casework. Puck lights suffer from uneven spotty distribution, while the linear LED illumination is much more even. Puck lights used in this situation would also produce glare, especially when someone is lying down in the bed. The linear LEDs are directed away from one's viewing angle, pointing instead toward the back of the casework. For this installation an LED source with a color temperature of 2400K (the color of dimmed incandescent) and a 90 CRI was used.

If this were a master bedroom, we might consider using a bedside lamp with an adjustable arm so that the lighting can be focused more precisely on the reading material and aimed away from the other person sharing the bed. But here a bedside table lamp performs admirably the task function for reading in bed. This lamp uses a translucent shade to defuse the light omnidirectionally. An opaque shade would project light only down and up. When selecting a shade for a table lamp, make sure you take the base with you. You can then immediately see if the shape and size is in scale with the base.

Bedrooms Project 2

Bedrooms have become more than places just for sleeping – they're our private sanctuaries from a stressful world. In this master bedroom the chaise lounge offers a cozy place to curl up with a book. The lighting in this room shows how to approach a luxurious more traditional interior design with a well-balanced mix of traditional luminaires and a flexible new application that can only be achieved with LEDs – the color tunable linear lighting.

During the day the frosted glass panels located behind the chest of drawers provide daylight from the bedroom windows to the master bath on the other side of the wall. At night they are illuminated with a perimeter run of linear LEDs that provides subtle visual interest at night. Like lighting providing illumination in skylight wells, this is another example of using daylight locations for electric lighting. The strip lighting is color tunable from 5000K down to 2150K, a color range that spans the full distance from daylight to candlelight.

Recessed adjustable low voltage downlights in the ceiling illuminate the ceramic pieces on the chest of drawers and in the curio niche behind the chaise lounge. The downlights are fitted with low voltage LED MR16 bulbs with a color temperature of 2700K and a CRI of 90.

The Asian inspired table lamps on the chest of drawers are purely decorative and like the sconces add visual interest and sparkle for the room These are fitted with a pleated silk shade, which softens the light source, a dimmable LED A-lamp with a CRI of 90 and a light output of 450 lumens. Because the LED bulb produces very little heat the shade will last much longer than if a standard 40W incandescent bulb were used.

The candlestick wall sconce is one of a pair which flank the curio niche. At 18" wide and 24" tall they might be considered over-scaled for the space, but visually they feel right. They use flame tip LED bulbs, with a color temperature of 2250K, the color of candlelight. Each bulb has an output of 225 lumens, which is equivalent to that of a 20W incandescent bulb. These bulbs only consume 3W worth of power, a savings of 85W per fixture. The sconces also provide a discreet soft ambient glow on the wall and ceiling. While LEDs are at a further remove from actual fire than even incandescent light sources, we want recognizable, reassuring forms partly out of nostalgia, but often for deeper more complex reasons. LEDs have proven themselves extremely flexible and adaptive to these somewhat retrograde but thoroughly modern applications. So when lighting more traditional interior designs, we can rely on traditional luminaire designs that very successfully employ LED light sources.

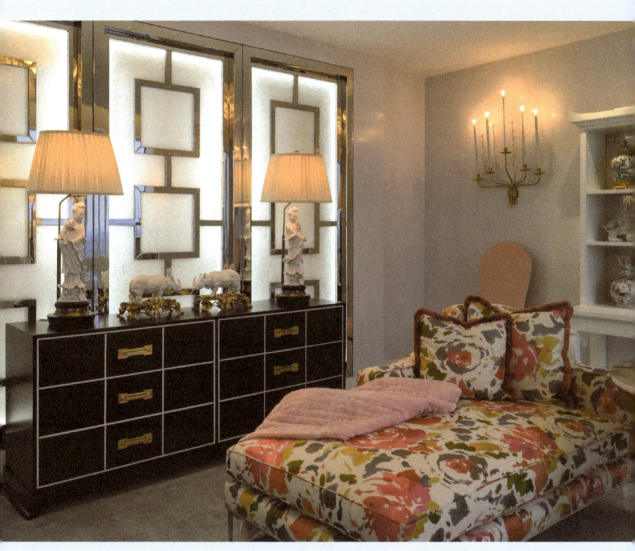

▲ Figure 16.4

Photos and Interior Design: Wright Simpkins, Lighting Design: Randall Whitehead.

CHAPTER 16 Bedrooms

Bedrooms Project 3

Bedrooms are not just purely functional anymore. They can have clean lines and be well lit or they can be sumptuous and a little over the top. This particular bedroom falls in that latter category – it's all about color, texture, and ambience.

In order to create this effect, a rectangular soffit was designed to run along the perimeter of the space. A crown molding on the interior edge of the soffit hides a run of linear LED lighting with a color temperature of 2400K and a CRI of 93. The rich amber color complements the muted browns of the wall covering and window shades. This indirect lighting also helps make the ceiling seem even taller than it actually is.

A sumptuous cast glass pendant fixture hangs in the center of the room, fitted with six dimmable LED A-lamps. Each bulb provides 800 lumens. These too, have a color temperature of 2400K. The fixture was originally designed to take six 60W incandescent bulbs, which would mean 360W worth of energy consumption. The LED versions provide the same lumen output but at a fraction of the energy cost – 7W each, for a total of 48W.

The bedside lamps have opaque shades which project light down toward the base of the lamp and onto reading surfaces. This also keeps them from overpowering the space, letting the floral-inspired pendant be the star of the room.

▲ Figure 16.5
Interior Design: Kristi Will Design, Lighting Design: Randall Whitehead.

Bedrooms Project 4

In this master bedroom, the bed floats in the center of the space, creating a different kind of openness which requires some thoughtful planning around the lighting. For instance, a flush-mounted floor plug was specified as part of the overall lighting plan so that floor lamps could be used as reading lights without running cords to the wall.

Adjustable recessed downlights with warm-dim capable integrated LED components installed in the ceiling direct light toward the art and the art objects placed around the room. A decorative pendant fixture in the left-hand corner made from a Vietnamese fish trap uses a globe-shaped LED bulb. Low-profile floor lamps over the bed have adjustable arms to provide flexible reading light and feature a touch control for three levels of light.

In the mirror we see a series of sliding shoji panels, which serve as the doors for the closets. Linear LED lights installed along the top of the closets provide illumination for the closet interior and backlighting for the shoji panels, adding a sense of depth to the room. The linear LED is color tunable, with a range between 5000K which shows how clothing will look during the day, and 2700K which shows how clothing will look in the evening.

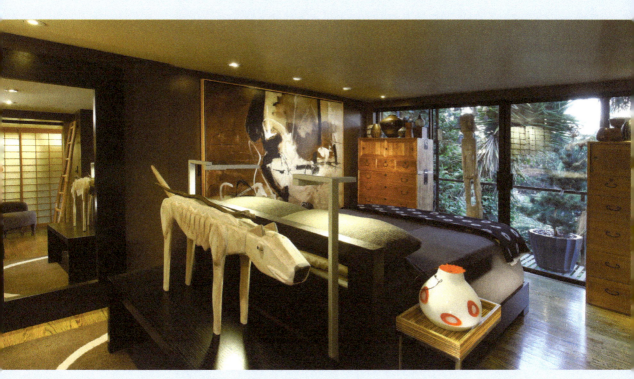

▲Figure 16.6

Photo: Dennis Anderson, Lighting Design: Randall Whitehead, Interior Design: Turner Martin.

▶ Figure 16.9

These days walk-in closets are often part of the master bedroom layout. Here linear LED lighting is installed vertically to evenly illuminate the purses and footwear displayed on the glass shelves. Photo: Robert Whitworth, Interior Design: Kristi Will Home + Design, Lighting Design: Randall Whitehead.

▲ Figure 16.7

Don't be conservative, think big when it comes to the ceiling luminaire. Adding a dropped ceiling in this concrete condominium provides enough plenum for adjustable recessed downlights and linear LED lighting. Photo: Christian Wright, Interior design: Wright Simpkins, Lighting design: Randall Whitehead.

◀ Figure 16.8

Photo: Dennis Anderson, Lighting Design: Randall Whitehead.

150   PART II Interior Lighting

Chapter 17

Entries

The entry to a home sets the scene for friends and visiting family members and should definitely convey a sense of welcome. This is where lighting plays a crucial role. Think of the entry as a tantalizing glimpse for visitors of what is to come. You want to look good when answering the door and for them to feel invited in. People are naturally drawn to light and good lighting in the entry unconsciously entices them to cross the threshold and come inside.

Like many rooms in the home, the default lighting solution in the entry is a decorative luminaire mounted at the center of the ceiling. If this is the only source of illumination it can tends to be relatively overly bright, creating glare. "Relatively" is the operative word in the last sentence; glare – the uncomfortable or even painful sensation of too much light – is experienced only in context. With no other light source in a room even a candle produces glare, and outdoors very high levels of light are not uncomfortable unless you look directly at the sun. Adding one or more light layers to a single ceiling mounted light source in the entry will create a more hospitable experience and a much better first impression.

Size Matters

Often people install decorative luminaires that are too small in scale for the room. When choosing luminaires, it's often difficult to judge if the sample luminaire you see in a lighting showroom or a big box store will be the right size, and it can be even harder to judge when shopping online. Websites and catalogs that show the luminaires installed so that you can see how they look in relationship to typical pieces of furniture can be very helpful. A good rule of thumb for selecting the correct size of a decorative ceiling luminaire for your entry (or for any room in your house) is to add the length and width of the room in feet and use this number in inches as the appropriate diameter of the luminaire. For example, if you have an entry that is 10' x 12' then your luminaire should be 22" in diameter. It's also OK to scale this up a bit and look for something in the 24" diameter range. If you have a low ceiling, choose a decorative luminaire that mounts close to the ceiling line. Even though it's tight to the ceiling that doesn't mean it has to be small. Be bold, go big.

▶ Figure 17.1

Photo: Dennis Anderson, Lighting Design: Randall Whitehead.

Don't Stop There

As mentioned above, the ceiling luminaire should not be the only source of illumination. Good lighting design involves light layering – in addition to decorative lighting you need other light layers such as accent lighting and ambient lighting.

Accent lighting highlights objects in the space such as art, tabletops, sculpture, and flower arrangements, creating the depth and dimension which is especially important for small entries. Accenting certain features with illumination pulls people in. Think of the entry as a little mini-gallery space (one of the case studies in this chapter is a full-on art gallery, decidedly un-mini). It's really a pass-through area that people linger in for a short amount of time, but it sets the tone for the rest of the house.

Recessed downlights are a standard way to provide the accent layer in entries, but consider using adjustable downlights so that you can direct the beam onto walls in addition to lighting objects – this amplifies the ambient layer and can avoid glare problems typical with downlights.

As in any other room in the house, ambient, or indirect, lighting is crucial to entries. Bouncing light off the ceiling softens shadows on people's faces. There are many ways to create ambient light in entries. A more architectural way is to install a cove lighting detail, on the wall, just below the ceiling line. Another way is to install wall sconces that are opaque that project light up toward the ceiling. A do-it-yourself way would be to purchase a pair of torchières (floor lamps with opaque shades).

The bottom line in entries is that if people look good, they feel good. And if cocktails are involved, everybody starts to look even better.

▶ Figure 17.2

Photo and Lighting Design: Randall Whitehead, Interior Design: Kristi Will Design + Home.

Entries Project 1

The entry creates the first impression of the home and doesn't need to be large in order to have impact. The one shown here is 12' by 12' with an 8' ceiling. The elongated hanging fixture that functions as a statement piece is actually a floor lamp suspended from the ceiling, made of wooden dowels and lined with a linen shade. This light column provides three light layers: decorative, ambient, and accent. It draws you into the room, provides fill light for the space, and projects light onto the blown glass disk placed on the pedestal below the fixture. The pedestal serves a second function – to prevent people from walking into the light fixture.

This statement piece fixture is rated to use four 60W household bulbs; instead it is fitted with four screw-in dimmable LED A-lamps at 8W apiece. The color temperature is 2400K with a CRI of 90. A pair of adjustable recessed downlights projects additional light onto the piece, adding another layer of shadowing and highlight.

Other adjustable recessed downlights highlight the art plants and furniture in the entry. A 26" tall wall sconce makes the ceiling seem higher than it actually is. It uses an 8W frosted LED T-lamp with a color temperature of 2200K and a CRI of 90.

The image on the right shows an alcove just off the entry that leads into the powder room and the guest room. The clear glass doors were sandblasted to give them the look of a shoji screen. When they are backlit, they add another welcoming layer of light into the space.

The back wall of the alcove is mirrored to help make this area seem wider. A perforated wooden screen placed in front breaks up the reflection so that it looks more like a passageway into another room instead of simply a mirror. The tall wooden sculpture in front is lit with an adjustable recessed downlight as well as an uplight built into its base.

▲ Figures 17.3, 17.4

Photos: Randall Whitehead and Lighting Design, Interior Design: Turner Martin Design.

▼ Figure 17.5

A serendipitous bonus effect was the shadows cast on the ceiling which come from light bouncing off the mirror and projecting it back through the wooden screen.

▼ Figure 17.6

A large piece of art hangs above a console table in the entry. A single adjustable recessed downlight illuminates the wall art as well as the wooden sculpture in front of it. This recessed fixture, along with the others, uses a 12V LED MR16 lamp with a color temperature of 2700K and a CRI of 90. These lamps are 11W each, replacing 50W halogen versions, and provide the same lumen output, higher light quality, and 80% energy savings.

CHAPTER 17 Entries

Entries Project 2

▶ Figure 17.7

Photo: Dennis Anderson, Lighting Design: Randall Whitehead.

As we indicated earlier in this chapter, the entry serves as a first impression of a home, and the owners of this one went all out to make sure everyone who visits is suitably impressed. It's almost as though the entry is the star of the show. The house was newly constructed, so it allowed for well-thought-out integration of lighting into the architecture. The house is built on a hill, so the architecture cascades downward – the highest point of the house is the entry, off the garage. The design team carefully considered the experiential sequence introduced to this house and the story it tells.

This entry is basically an art gallery, and one where not only is the art illuminated, but the illumination itself is art. The real showstopper is a 40' light installation that runs the length of the entry hall. A 9" wide by 2" deep recess has been built into the ceiling. Hanging 12" down from the recess is a shallow metal trough which is also 9" wide by 2" deep. Inside this trough is a run of RGBW color changing linear lighting. It projects colored light into the recess, so that appears to be glowing. RGBW stands for red, green, blue, white which are the color of the LED diodes, which can be mixed to create thousands of colors and patterns. These are programmed to change gradually over a long period of time, instead of changing abruptly from one color to the next, and are also connected to the sound system, allowing the light display to change in rhythm to music.

▶ Figures 17.8, 17.9, 17.10

This series of images shows some of the many patterns of light that can be created with full color tunable LEDs. All of the lighting throughout the house is tied into a smart house system. There are controls located at each of the doors, but the lighting can also be changed using a phone or a voice command. The owners travel quite a bit, so the lighting is set to come on at different times in various rooms throughout the evening – alternating the lighting each day makes it appear that someone is in the house.

A view from the outside of the house shows how the entry is really a bridge with a wall of glass on one side, leading from the garage and front door into the main part of the house as it works its way down the hill. Uplighting from below illuminates the large live oak. Balancing interior and exterior lighting this way creates a unity in a home and avoids the black mirror effect of windows at night.

The view of the front of the house as seen from the street draws the eye to the welcoming glow of the front door, made of orange cast glass. Adjustable recessed downlights in the overhang and in the ceiling of the entry behind the door backlight the door from both the exterior and the interior. The downlights have a color temperature of 2700K with a CRI of 90, and the exterior ones are damp location rated.

In line with the overhang are a pair of horizontal windows that bring natural light into the two closets flanking the front door. At night, they are illuminated from within, acting as architecturally integrated modern lanterns.

▶ Figures 17.11, 17.12

Photos: Dennis Anderson, Lighting Design, Randall Whitehead.

Entries Project 3

▶ Figure 17.13

Photo: Matthew Millman, Lighting Design: Anna Kondolf, Interior Design: Kristi Will Home + Design.

In entries, sometimes architecture is the big event. In this case, a chandelier, art, or furniture are all unnecessary. As guests come through the front door they are entranced with this very sculptural spiral staircase, which leads them up to the main living space level.

There is a round skylight at the top of the staircase which fills this area with natural light during the day. At night, cool colored LED lighting, installed within the lightwell, continues to enhance the hand-painted cloud mural.

The stair treads are made of cast glass. Each one is illuminated by a run of LED linear lighting recessed into the wall. The cast glass pieces can be lifted out if the lighting needs to be serviced

The stair lighting is part of a control system that dims the intensity of the lighting as dusk approaches.

Entries Project 4

▶ Figure 17.14

Photo: Ken Rice, Lighting Design: Randall Whitehead.

This project is a "what's-wrong-with-this-picture" exercise. Yes, this entry is dramatic. It makes for a great photograph, but in real life could use some upgrading. If you're an aspiring or practicing designer, dramatic photographs may get you more work and increase your sense of your own fabulousness, but the real-life experience of your clients is more important.

On the plus side, we have two strong contrasting colors that play off of each other. The bronze bowl filled with moss is illuminated by a single recessed downlight overhead that uses an LED MR16 90 CRI 3000K lamp fitted with a green filter to intensify the color. Using a low pedestal in the center of the room, as opposed to a taller entry table, gives additional interest and allows for a clear view through the entry into the rest of the house. The red lacquer Chinese cabinet adds a strong vertical element and another pop of vibrant color. The cinnabar red chest and emerald green foliage take the place of more traditional art. Two recessed adjustable downlights illuminate the art glass placed on top of the cabinet. A piece of 36" x 18" white paper has been placed on top of the piece to reflect light up onto the ceiling.

Even with these clever effects, somehow the lighting is not quite enough. What's wrong exactly? This is an example of the "museum effect," where objects are more important than the people occupying the space or the interior architecture. This is how museums traditionally used to light their collections – bright dramatic spot lighting on the artwork without any additional light for the walls or ceilings. This can cause a lot of eye fatigue. As you go from gallery to gallery your eyes try to adjust between the illuminated art pieces and the dark walls that surround them. Museums are now adding a lot more ambient light so that the contrast between the art and the walls is greatly reduced.

The ambient light layer is what this entry needs most. Without it, the room appears smaller and the ceiling feels lower. There are several ways that fill light can be added. One option would be to place torchière lamps (floor lamps with opaque shades that project light toward the ceiling) on either side of the cabinet. Another option would be to add a cantilevered shelf detail, mounted 9" down from the ceiling line, with a run of LED linear lighting. A good choice for color temperature would be 2400K with a CRI of 95. The linear lighting could be placed in an aluminum extrusion that positions it so that the light comes out at a 45° angle, pushing more light toward the center of the room.

Adding a layer of ambient light will help make this foyer feel more welcoming without sacrificing the drama provided by the accent lights. Following this tip will also make you even more amazing as a designer than you already are!

◀Figure 17.15

Lighting a tall entry can be challenge. Select a hanging fixture that is long enough to visually connect the two stories without having any light bulbs glaring into people's eyes from above or below. Photo: Jeff Zaruba, Lighting and Interior Design: Turner Martin.

▲Figure 17.16

This oval-shaped staircase becomes even more dramatic at night as each tread is illuminated with 2200K linear LED lighting. A routed channel, located below the nosing of each of the stairs, provides a space for a subtle and seamless installation. Photo: Sid Espinoza.

▼Figure 17.17

This delightful LED pendant adds lively visual interest to the entry. Photo: Randall Whitehead.

Chapter 18

Open Plan Spaces

The term "open plan" simply means that you have a large open space where different areas flow together. Often the term "great room" is used to convey the same concept, albeit with a certain degree of baronial pretense, as though you are referring to your massive hunting lodge or ancestral castle. Open plan multipurpose rooms began to appear in modernist homes built by Joseph Eichler in California in the 1950s and 1960s, and developers started building high-end houses with great rooms in the 1970s and 1980s. Great rooms then became a nearly ubiquitous feature of suburban homes constructed in America in the 1990s and 2000s.

The challenge with this room type from the standpoint of lighting and interior design is to create a sense of separation for the different areas. A good lighting control system can help here by offering separate dimming and scenes for the living room, dining room, and kitchen.

▶ Figure 18.1

Photo: Dennis Anderson, Lighting Design: Randall Whitehead.

Start with the Kitchen

Typical open plan spaces today include an open kitchen with a large island facing out toward the rest of the great room, with a workspace on one side and seating for family or casual entertaining on the other. From the kitchen you can see the living room and dining room areas, and vice versa.

The kitchen requires more light, especially task light, than the other areas. It also needs a whiter (cooler color temperature) light for food preparation and cleaning. This is where warm-dim LEDs work very well – allowing you the flexibility to change color temperature from cool daylight all the way down to warm candlelight. After a meal is prepared and the entertaining has begun, the kitchen illumination can be dimmed down and warmed up so that it doesn't visually overpower the other areas.

Get That Glow

When designing lighting for an open plan space, it's good to start with a plan on how to create the ambient light layer. A shelf or cantilever can be integrated into the walls or ceiling to provide a hiding place for indirect lighting. Depending on the depth, this architectural detail can also hold vents for the HVAC system or reveals for roller shades. This is especially

beneficial for sloped or pitched ceilings because it keeps a large volume of space from falling into shadow while highlighting architectural details such as beams or trusses.

With a pitched ceiling with support trusses that run parallel to the floor, indirect lighting can be installed on top of those horizontal beams. A series of opaque sconces can also be used to project light toward the ceiling. Another technique that can be used instead of or in combination with these methods is to use pendant luminaires or chandeliers that provide both ambient light as well as a decorative element to the space. These ambient/decorative luminaires can also add a more human scale to the room.

On projects with more modest budgets or for rental spaces, torchières (floor lamps) with opaque shades open at the top can be used, and easily repositioned, to provide the ambient layer of illumination.

▶ Figure 18.2

Photo and Lighting Design: Randall Whitehead, Interior Design: Turner Martin Design.

Decorative As Task

Floor lamps, pharmacy lamps, and table lamps all fulfill the decorative layer as well as task light for reading, knitting, and other activities. They create little islands of illumination that draw people into various seating areas.

Accent lighting, used to highlight objects in the space, can come from recessed adjustable recessed downlights, track lighting, rail systems, or bridge systems. Remember, don't use this light to illuminate seating areas. It will cast harsh shadows on people's faces.

Open Plan Spaces Project 1

▶ Figures 18.3, 18.4

Photos: Drew Kelly, Lighting Design: Techlinea, Architect: Geddes Ulinskas, Interior Design: Kendall Wilkinson.

Often the challenge of an open plan design is to create a sense of more intimate areas within the large space. This condominium layout contains two seating areas which are open to the entry and the dining room beyond. The two glowing pendant fixtures with incorporated LED linear lighting help to define the two seating areas. The recessed adjustable low voltage LED fixtures, controlled in separate groups, also help distinguish these as separate areas.

A shallow soffit runs along the entire perimeter of the space. A cantilever detail hides the linear LED lighting. These light emitting diodes have color changing capabilities. There are red, green, blue, and white diodes; they can be mixed together through a controller which is part of the dimming system to create a huge variety of color variations, including the rich warm hue seen in the image. The soffit detail performs other functions as well. It houses the vents for the HVAC system, as well as recessed troughs for the motorized shades.

The fireplace wall has wide vertical strips of burnished metal. In between them are narrow bands of white opal Plexiglas which have been backlit with color changing LEDs.

Placed very subtly around the room are low profile pharmacy lamps which give reading light without drawing attention to themselves, as would a shaded floor lamp.

Open Plan Spaces Project 2

▶ Figures 18.5, 18.6

Photos and Lighting Design: Randall Whitehead Interior Design: Turner Martin.

This open plan layout combines the living room and dining room areas. The owners are avid art collectors so a flexible layout of adjustable recessed downlights was installed in the ceiling so that the art objects and paintings could be moved around. The downlights use 12V MR 16 11.5W lamps, which provide a lumen output of 700–800 per lamp. Lamps with this greater output were necessary since the ceiling is high, sloping upward from 12' to 18'. Three of them graze the façade of the fireplace, raking light across the textured surface. Two other adjustable recessed downlights focus attention on the pinwheel inspired metal sculpture on the dining room table and cast interesting shadows.

A discreetly elegant pharmacy reading lamp with a shielded shade and bronze finish by the sofa does its job well while blending in perfectly with the other elements of the room

This raised area opens onto an inner courtyard and features doors flanked by a colonnade of bronze and blown glass sconces. These decorative luminaires are 12" wide and 36" tall. These dimensions may seem perhaps overscale at first, but within the envelope of the architecture are definitely the right size. Insets have been designed into the columns, so the luminaires do not project too far into the walkway. Along the front face of the soffit, located above the walkway, are a series of indirect wall sconces with asymmetric reflectors which throw light out across the ceiling to create the ambient light for the space.

Open Plan Spaces Project 3

▶ Figures 18.7, 18.8

Photos: Russell Abraham,
Architecture: Lindy Small.

Outdoor rooms are also very much open plan spaces that can become part of the everyday living environment, with the help of proper lighting. The design for this home includes two patio areas allocated for alfresco dining and seating, which are seamlessly integrated in an open floor plan. The whole main floor area has a wonderful inviting glow. Most of this comes from a cantilevered shelf detail which runs along the entire length of the back wall. Linear LED lighting is installed on top of the shelf, housed in a triangular extrusion with a frosted lens. The light is projected out at a 45° angle in order to wash a wide surface area of the ceiling. This has a color temperature of 2700K with a CRI of 93.

Half cylinder-shaped opaque wall sconces throw light both up and down. These luminaires provide two functions. The first is to create ambient illumination for the exterior dining and seating areas by that washing light out across the overhang, connecting the interior and exterior areas visually and enhancing the architectural flow of the building. The second is to create a secondary ceiling line. The actual ceiling soars from 10' to 18', and wall sconces are mounted at 10' on center, carrying the visual line of the 10' ceiling out to the exterior rooms. This is a strong example of how lighting not only provides illumination but helps to articulate architectural form.

Adjustable recessed downlights are installed in four primary rows. They have square trims, which tie into the architectural lines of the building much better than round versions. They feature a rotation of 358°, with an aiming angle of 45° to highlight the tabletops, art, and sculpture. This wide range adjustability on the downlights helps the floor plan be more fluid, allowing furniture to be moved around freely. We advocate strongly for adjustable versions whenever you need to use downlights – if these were fixed downlights you would simply see a row of circular beam spreads hitting the furniture and floor. It is best not to have recessed downlights over seating areas as they can create harsh shadows on people's faces. It's better to focus them on art and other surfaces that would benefit from accent lighting or use them for wall washing to illuminate vertical surfaces.

The recessed downlights are divided into five switching groups, along with separate controls for the wall sconces and the indirect lighting. These are all tied into the dimming system, allowing the homeowners to create lighting scenes. These scenes can be preset, so with a touch of a button, the lighting can transition from bright and cheery to intimate and cozy.

Open Plan Spaces Project 4

▶ Figures 18.9, 18.10

Photos: Dennis Anderson, Lighting Design: Randall Whitehead, Interior Design: Kristi Will Design + Home.

Pendant luminaires are good way of creating a sense of separation between the different areas of an open plan layout. In this open area, we see three defined spaces within the floor plan. The decorative luminaires do a good job of giving the living room, dining room, and kitchen their own personalities.

In the foreground, a large drum-shaped pendant hangs above the living room area. Adjustable recessed downlights project light onto the coffee table. Within the skylight opening, indirect opaque wall sconces create the ambient light for this gathering space. This is an excellent example of using the function of an architectural element – the skylight opening – to do double duty for both day and night illumination. When thinking about lighting at night, it is often useful to see how a space is lit by daylight during the day. In fact, this project demonstrates a masterful balance of daylight and electric light.

Indirect lighting has been installed on top of the casework holding the television monitor. Each of the shelves has linear LED lighting mounted at the front, hidden by the 2" wood trim. The color temperature of the LED linear lighting is 2400K; this is true of all of the LED linear lighting in the space. The recessed adjustable downlights have a color temperature of 2700K. Both light sources have a CRI of 90.

The kitchen features two blown glass pendant luminaires which are spaced evenly above the eat-in island. Ambient light is installed on top of the kitchen casework. Below the cabinets additional linear LED lighting, on a separate dimming control, provides nearly shadow-free task light for the countertop. One more run of LED linear light is installed on the underside of the island countertop where the chairs are tucked in, keeping the niche from becoming a dark recess at night.

The dining room has five pendant luminaires hanging at different lengths above the table. Adjustable recessed downlights installed also light the art on the walls.

Wall sconces which are installed around the perimeter of the open plan help unify the spaces. They also create a secondary ceiling line that adds some intimacy to this expansive floor plan.

Each of the areas has its own control system, accessed from the main doors that lead into this first floor space. In addition, a wireless remote allows for people to lower the lighting to watch a movie without having to get up to access a wall controller.

▲ Figure 18.11

Photo: Dennis Anderson, Lighting Design: Randall Whitehead.

▶ Figure 18.12

Photo: Russell Abraham, Lighting Design: Randall Whitehead, Interior Design: Schippmann Design.

Part III | Exterior Lighting

Overview

The purpose of this section is to familiarize you with the many techniques used for lighting exterior residential spaces and gardens. The four light layers – task, ambient, accent, and decorative – apply here as well. Decorative luminaires include lanterns mounted on the façade of the main house and outbuildings; pole lamps; and luminaires hanging inside gazebos, pergolas, and sometimes even from the trees. Accent luminaires include directional lights used to illuminate trees, ground cover, water features, and sculpture. Task luminaires include pathway lights and stair lights to get family and guests safely from area to area. The ambient layer outdoors can come from string lights suspended above a seating area, light bounced off the ceilings or walls of exterior structures. In the right conditions, a very subtle beautiful ambient layer can also be created by uplighting tree canopies.

The world of outdoor lighting has really opened up now, and LEDs provide capabilities in lighting that were never possible before. People are discovering how to use exterior spaces as a way of expanding their interior spaces. When the weather is good, there is nothing better than a little relaxation time outside. Not everyone has a giant backyard or front yard – sometimes it's only a little postage stamp garden, a small concrete patio area, or simply a balcony. Whatever the space is, it becomes usable at night with the addition of lighting. If it's a large space, lighting can help create more intimate areas for gatherings, spaces that come to be seen as "outdoor rooms."

The entry door, front façade, and lawn area are important. Like they say, "You only get one chance to make a good first impression." This is something that will be addressed in this section.

Another big advantage of exterior lighting is that it makes interior spaces seem larger because instead of seeing yourself reflected in the black mirror of a dark window, your eye travels outward through the glass and out into the well-lit foliage beyond. People also feel a little bit safer in their homes when they can see what is outside if they hear a noise.

The bottom line is that these exterior spaces are valuable real estate and their use is increased when they're illuminated properly.

▶ Figure EXT.1

Photo: Russell Abraham,
Architecture: Lindy Small.

Chapter 19

Exterior Spaces

Be Street Smart

How a house looks at night from the street says a lot about the people inside. To begin with, security lighting is the opposite of good exterior or landscape lighting. Harsh lights, mounted under the eaves of the house, glaring out at people are simply not welcoming, especially when activated by motion sensors. The message is not "Welcome, come on in," it's more like "Halt, who goes there?" Also consider having some illumination behind the windows at the front of the house, as a part of the landscape controls. If left dark black the windows will resemble jack-o' lanterns in which the candles have gone out – not very inviting.

Make sure to light the yard area all the way from the sidewalk to the front door in order to increase the sense of depth to the property. Similarly, make sure that there is some lighting to the far right and the far left of the property so that it looks as wide as possible. When it comes real estate, size does matter.

You can't put in a row of pagoda lights, eight prepackaged accent lights, a pole lantern at the bottom of the driveway, and a sconce or two at the front door and call it a day. Consider all light layers – task, accent, ambient, and decorative – on the exterior just as you would do inside the house. Good exterior lighting design feels natural but takes a lot of work and a good understanding of how to use and balance light layers.

The Task Layer

A primary function of task lighting outdoors, which includes pathway and step lighting, is to help people get from the street safely up to the front door. Direct light sources should be shielded from the eye so that they cast light down along the planting areas that border the pathways. Traditional pagoda lights can visually overpower the surrounding landscape as their brightness draws attention to the light fixture instead of what they are supposed to be illuminating.

The Accent Layer

The accent light layer in the exterior of the home highlights plantings, sculptures, water features, and architectural details. Accent luminaires are

▶ Figures 19.1, 19.2

Photos: Dennis Anderson, Lighting Design: Randall Whitehead.

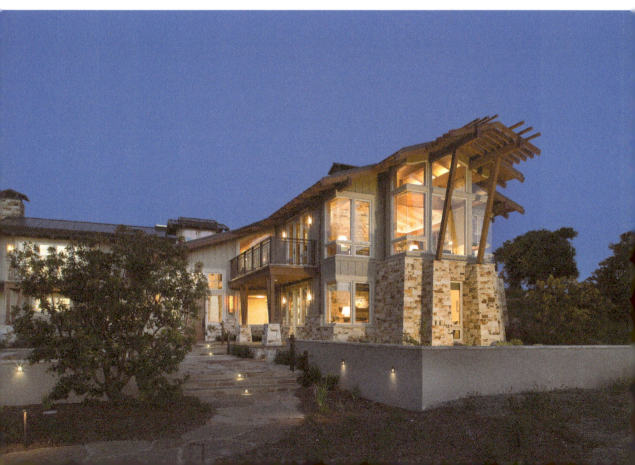

typically directional and can be mounted in the ground, in trees, or on buildings. They can also throw a soft grazing of light along the facade of the house to pick up the texture of the building material. You want your house to look like it's being discovered among the trees, rather than like a billboard on the freeway.

Uplighting in the exterior can be very effective, but usually needs to be balanced with other layers. A combination of uplighting and downlighting in trees can be very effective and can create a dappled pattern of light and shadow onto planter beds, pathways, and outdoor areas. This is called moonlighting, the effect you get when a full moon creates shadows.

▶ Figure 19.3

Photo and Lighting Design: Randall Whitehead.

The Decorative Layer

Modern and traditional decorative LED luminaires rated for exterior use, including pole lanterns, sconces, and pendants, are widely available. You can hang a decorative luminaire over the dining table, whether it's inside the gazebo, in the cabana or under a tree, creating an outdoor "room."

The Ambient Layer

The ambient layer plays a role outside in creating a comfortable relaxing sense of an outdoor room. There are many ways to create the ambient layer outdoors, including bouncing light off gazebo ceilings, or the underside of eaves or even umbrellas. Indirect lighting for the front porch or entryway draws people up to the front door and softens the shadows. And lighting the underside of mature tree canopies can be a magical way to convey a sense of enclosure.

Another way to create ambient light is to use rows of LED string lights suspended above the entertaining areas. These create the sense of the ceiling line and provide a diffuse, flattering light for both guests and family members.

Size and Whispers

Exterior luminaires, such as pendant lights above the front door, sconces flanking the entry, or decorative fixtures in the garage area, must be the right scale when seen from the street. Think of them as architectural earrings from the Cher collection – clearly visible from a distance. Judging the true size of luminaires you're considering from cut sheets or online catalogs can be difficult. When in doubt, get a sample luminaire, or use a cardboard mockup, and test it on site, viewing from the street to judge its size in context.

Exterior Ratings

LED light sources, whether integrated components or standalone lamps, are now widely available with exterior ratings. This means different things for lamps (or bulbs) than it does for luminaires (or fixtures). For lamps that are used in enclosed exterior luminaires, the rating is "for enclosed fixtures," which means that the lamp won't overheat in the fixture. (LEDS are cooler than incandescent light sources but still generate heat.) "Integral" luminaires suitable for exterior use have two different ratings – "wet rated" and "damp rated."

Color and Output

Exterior lighting has traditionally color temperatures in the 3000° Kelvin range, the color of halogen light sources, as warmer temperatures can make plants look sickly. But at night, temperatures above 3000K are generally not preferred. When lighting hardscape (non-plant materials), choose a color temperature that complements the areas or materials you are illuminating. Redwood and sandstone are more enhanced by a warmer color temperature (2700K), while gray granite and river rock look better under a slightly cooler color temperature (3000K).

Most LEDs used in exterior luminaires dim in intensity but don't change color temperature, which is an advantage over halogen light sources, which get warmer when dimmed. In general though you're probably not going to need to dim most exterior lights, as in the garden and yard at night, a little light goes a long way. A 70' tall tree can be fully illuminated with two 700 lumen LED MR16 uplights, for instance.

LEDs for exterior lighting with high color rendering have not traditionally been in high demand, although this is changing, and high color rendering is gradually becoming more standard across all LED products. But use the highest color rendering light sources you can find when possible; even for exterior purposes it still matters.

Exterior Spaces Project 1

▶ Figure19.4

Photo: Misha Bruk, Lighting Design: Randall Whitehead.

This garden showcases a Balinese teahouse. The Balinese style teahouse differs from the Japanese style because it has glass on three sides and one solid wall, whereas a Japanese tea house would have shoji panels instead of glass. Glass protects occupants from insects and inclement weather but allows a full view of the garden, and shoji panels are fitted with a translucent material that allow in light when closed, but those inside cannot see out.

The main house is located two stories above the garden (notice the windows in the upper left-hand corner) For this reason the garden needed to be illuminated so that it could be seen from above.

If you look closely you can pick out the exterior rated low-voltage accent lights. The original 12V halogen MR16 lamps were replaced with LED versions. Each original accent light with halogen lamps used 50W, while the LED replacements only use 11W but have the same lumen output.

The staircase leading from the second floor of the house down into the garden is illuminated evenly with a continuous run of exterior rated LED linear lighting, mounted on the underside of the left-hand rail. A 2-inch wood trim shields the light from view as people descend or ascend the stairs. The exterior rated accent light mounted above the door exiting the house projects light onto an evergreen planted next to the stairs. The second exterior rated accent light, mounted on the back side of the railing, highlights a collection of succulents and bromeliads.

Inside the teahouse, a pair of continuous runs of exterior rated LED linear lighting project illumination upwards onto the two-tiered ceiling. The color temperature is 2400K with a CRI of 95. This color of light enhances the warmth of the wood and helps draw people into the space. From the center of the ceiling hangs a 30" wide organically shaped pendant luminaire resembling a huge magnolia blossom. It uses a dimmable, single screw-base 8W LED A-lamp with a color temperature of 2700K and CRI of 90.

Exterior rated accent lights are mounted up under the eaves of the teahouse as well as below the footing. The high mounted fixtures throw an even wash of illumination onto the ground cover plantings and walkway. The lower fixtures project light up into the trees and shrubbery.

The landscape lighting is controlled by a wireless system, using handheld controls located at the door of the house, that leads down to the garden and inside the teahouse.

A detail shot of the garden shows how the illumination from the teahouse is utilized. The uplighting accents the Japanese maple in the foreground, along with the large pottery vessels in the background. The downlighting brings out the color and texture of the lush ground cover. A cooler color temperature of 3000K was selected to enhance the greens of the plantings, and the 90 CRI keeps the colors from going flat.

▶ Figure 19.5–19.7

Photos: Misha Bruk, Lighting Design: Randall Whitehead.

Exterior Spaces Project 2

The challenge on this project was to come up with a lighting design that produced a sense of presence for a house that sits so far back from the sidewalk. The first step was to add some illumination at the garage doors. The large-scale lantern, in keeping with the architecture of the house, projects outward from the facade and helps to guide people to the front door as they stroll off the sidewalk. This luminaire uses four exterior rated LED flame tip lamps at 2400 K with a CRI of 90, creating the look of a dimmed incandescent light source. Two recessed exterior rated LED downlights are mounted in each of the two arches above the garage doors, creating little pools of light that project out onto the sidewalk.

From the street, you can see the arched windows of the living room and the rectangular windows of the master bedroom located on the floor above. These rooms, as well as the rest of the house, are filled with a pleasant glow of ambient light at night. The living room windows virtually disappear behind trees during the day but come into full view at night.

In between the two sets of windows are a series of five friezes. They are illuminated from below, using accent lights mounted on an 18" arm extension. Each fixture has an exterior rated 5W LED lamp which provides illumination equal to that of a 20W halogen.

The front garden, located on top of the garage, uses exterior rated LED ground mounted accent lights to highlight the foliage. They are tied in with step lights mounted 12" above the stair treads on 3' centers. The exterior rated lantern on the far right acts as another visual signpost for guests.

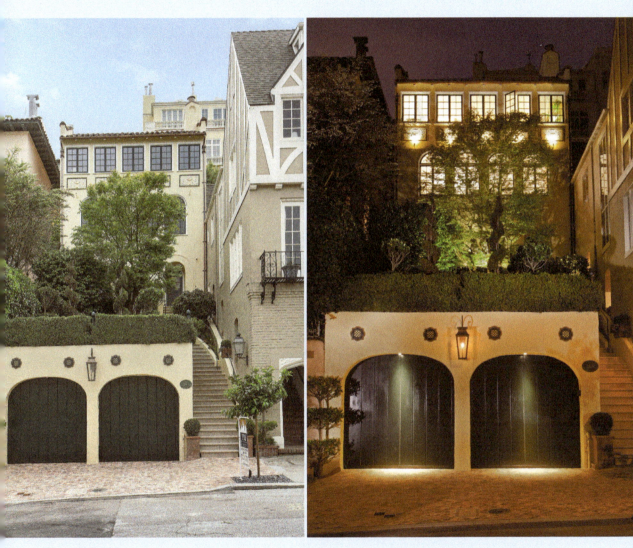

▲ Figures 19.8, 19.9

Photos: Dennis Anderson, Lighting Design: Randall Whitehead.

CHAPTER 19 Exterior Spaces

Exterior Spaces Project 3

▶ Figure 19.10-19.12

Photos: Dennis Anderson, Lighting Design: Randall Whitehead.

Much of the time we view our gardens from inside the house through the windows, because it's too hot or too cold outside ... or there are too many bugs. In order for us to be able to see the garden from inside we need balanced light both inside and out, which means having a strong layer of illumination to combat the darkness. This patio and garden area has luminaires within the planting areas as well as the facade of the house.

Exterior rated accent lights, mounted on the back wall of the residence, are located 18" above the 8' sliding glass doors that lead out to the garden and throw a strong wash of illumination over the greenery. This is not a comfortable light for when the family is entertaining outside, but is used specifically for viewing the garden from within the house. Therefore, these luminaires are switched separately from the other lights. The luminaries have an integrated LED component with a color temperature of 3000K and a CRI of 95 and an output of 1100 lumens, (equal a 75W incandescent reflector bulb) but use only 16.5W. Four fixtures in total are installed above the doors.

Tucked within the plantings are adjustable exterior rated accent lights, which add depth and dimension to the garden. They uplight the Australian tree ferns, along with tall conifers at the far back of the garden (not visible in this shot). These are the lights that would be used when people are outside – they don't have to be so bright because they're not competing with the lighting inside the house. The 3000K, 95 CRI LEDs enhance the vibrant colors of the landscaping.

This is a daylight shot of the garden. Here, the conifers can be seen at the back. This is a small urban city garden that has been terraced to create a sense of greater depth. While it is beautiful during the day, it would fall into complete darkness at night without the use of landscape lighting, and the windows facing the garden would become "black mirrors" at night, reflecting the light from within the room and obscuring the ability to see outside.

This closeup of one of the adjustable ground mounted accent light shows how well they integrate into the garden, even during the day. This particular luminaire was specified with a powder coat bronze finish. Many manufacturers offer these luminaires in a variety of finishes, including a marine grade version for projects located near the ocean. Marine grade fixtures are fabricated from bronze, brass, or copper, metals that hold up well against the corrosive effects of salt air.

Exterior Spaces Project 4

In many parts of the world people can enjoy alfresco living when the weather is good. Outdoor living is a big part of the culture in Hawaii all year round. Many homes, like this one, create outdoor rooms. Yes, this one is gigantic, but even smaller Hawaiian homes have lanais where family gatherings are a constant. Along the back of this house are two seating areas located under a deep overhang which provides shelter in wet weather. Off to the right, a little further out, is the dining area located in an open-air pavilion next to the pool. Note that the underwater lights are located on the house side of the pool – if they were located on the opposite side they would glare into people's eyes. These luminaries are color tunable. The owners can pick out a hue of illumination that suits their liking for the occasion.

Well lights, recessed into the outer edge of the deck, project light up to illuminate the overhang and produce ambient light. They are fitted with deep louvers that hide the light source. These fixtures have dimmable, exterior rated, LED components that produce 1600 lumens, a color temperature of 2700K and a CRI of 90.

Large-scale sconces are installed on the four walls sections of the facade. When picking out decorative fixtures it's best to do an elevation to determine what size looks best. When in doubt, go a little larger instead of smaller. This also helps determine where the junction box should be installed. Sometimes the backplate of a fixture has the power feed right in the center, but other times it may be located at the top or the bottom. These sconces use four low wattage LED filament lamps, have a color temperature of 2200K and a CRI of 90.

Directional accent lights are attached to the support beams of the overhang. They illuminate tabletops, outdoor art, and plants. These are landscape fixtures that have been adapted for a surface mount installation. Marine grade luminaries were selected in order to hold up against the elements.

The dining pavilion sports a large pendant fixture that looks like a giant chrysanthemum. It is made of thin slices of coconut shell that have been painted white.

The front yard area of the house feels serene and contemplative. A wide wooden walkway appears to float over a reflecting pond filled with water lilies and koi. The granite monoliths located off to the right are fountains whose water spills into the pond. Waterproof submersible fixtures are tucked in below to provide accent lighting at night, and pathway lights help guide visitors to the front door after dark.

The front of the house uses a series of Japanese inspired wall sconces to draw people towards the building. The two lanterns flanking the front door are larger in scale than the others to help define this as the entryway.

▲ Figure 19.13

Photo: Dennis Anderson, Interior Design: Wright Simpkins.

▲ Figure 19.14

Photo: Dennis Anderson, Interior Design: Wright Simpkins.

▲ Figure 19.15

A comparison daylight shot shows how well-done lighting creates a magical landscape at night. Photo: Dennis Anderson, Interior Design: Wright Simpkins.

CHAPTER 19 Exterior Spaces

Exterior Spaces Project 5

The landscaping of this Scottsdale, Arizona property, which includes a main house and a guest house, is in concert with the natural landscaping of its desert setting. The pool has a natural shape built around boulders existing on the property. Most of the year it is too hot during the day to enjoy the garden, but the evenings are the perfect temperature for outdoor eating and entertaining. The design of this house requires a subtle approach to lighting which complements the blending of nature and habitat. It is a good example of how light sources can be artfully concealed so that all you see is what's being illuminated. This is the essence of good exterior lighting design. The effect is natural and unforced, but takes a lot of planning, coordination, and collaboration with architects and other team members, perhaps the most important part of the design process.

The large madrone tree located between the two buildings is the centerpiece of the yard. The outer canopy of foliage is illuminated from exterior rated, directional accent lights mounted on the roofs of the two structures. They use an 11W LED M16 lamp with a color temperature of 3000K and a CRI of 90, with the lumen output of a 50W halogen lamp. These luminaires are fitted with a 2.5" snoot that acts as a baffle in order to hide the light source from view. There are also four exterior rated, ground mounted directional luminaires near the base of the tree that project light up the trunk and into the center of the canopy. Note: Not all LED lamps work well in enclosed light luminaires. Make sure that the ones you select are rated for such use.

Other exterior rated, directional accent lights are mounted in the branches of the madrone tree and are directed downwards, illuminating the lower planting areas and pathways. As the light passes through the lower branches from the upper branches it casts shadows onto the ground, creating a moonlighting effect.

Lighting for ground cover and pathways near the guest house comes from directional luminaires that are mounted on the back side of the pergola cast horizontal beams. Two perforated metal lanterns hang over the guest house porch and use clear filament LED A-lamps with a color temperature of 2400K and a CRI of 90. The light passing through the perforated metal casts a pattern of light onto the walls and ceiling of the porch.

Pathway luminaires, located in the further reaches of the yard, are shielded so that they project light downward. These luminaires use a 3W LED source with a color temperature of 3000K and a CRI of 90.

The wall sconces on the main house are opaque, projecting light up and down and not in your face. In low light situations, the effect created by a lantern with clear or frosted glass can be too glaring.

▲ Figure 19.16

Photo: Eric Zaruba, Lighting Design: Randall Whitehead, Interior Design: Turner Martin Design.

▲ Figure 19.17

Photo: Eric Zaruba, Lighting Design: Randall Whitehead, Interior Design: Turner Martin Design.

▶ Figure 19.18

Photo: Randall Whitehead.

▲Figure 19.19

Colored laser lights can create the look of hundreds of small lights hanging from tree branches. Photo and Lighting Design: Randall Whitehead.

▼Figure 19.20

These stairs use a LED linear lighting which is mounted on the underside of the nosings. The warm light (2400K, 90 CRI) enhances the wood tones. Photo: Randall Whitehead.

▲Figure 19.21

Giant Argonite crystals have been hollowed out so that lighting can be installed. During the day, they look quite natural, but at night they have a fiery glow. Photo: Randall Whitehead.

▼Figure 19.22

This dramatic entry is grand but inviting. It's an excellent example of well-balanced light layering and concealing the light sources so that the eye only focuses on the architecture. Photo: © Douglas A. Salin, Lighting Design: Randall Whitehead, Interior Design: Bethe Cohen and Associates.

Part IV | Design Details

Chapter 20

Design Details

Light is a visual medium, but unlike other materials it is ephemeral and elusive. Still, understanding and communicating details about equipment, connections, locations, specifications, and hardware is an important part of lighting design – all top lighting designers learn this art and craft well.

With these diagrams and drawings, we want to show some techniques that are better explained in schematic detail. These are quick references to explain how lighting effects are produced. Sometimes schematic drawings and diagrams are expedient way of getting a concept across to a client, a contractor, or a loved one.

In design, the goal is usually for lighting to be unobtrusive and integrated into the architecture and interior design as much as possible. You want the positive effects of the lighting to be seen and felt, but not the luminaires themselves, except for the decorative ones. Again, this is why it is so important for lighting designers to get involved in the design process as early as possible and to work closely with the other team members, especially the architects. Think of these schematic drawings as visual shorthand for communicating abstract ideas.

These design details represent techniques that you will be using over and over again. Sharing these with your clients, contractor, or your significant other will help move the lighting design process along.

▶ Figure 20.1

Photo: Dennis Anderson, Lighting Design: Randall Whitehead.

Lighting Ceilings

Figure 20.2: Making use of a high sloped ceiling and a luminaire mounted high on a wall to produce a full ambient light layer.

Figure 20.3: Structural beams can be used to locate linear LEDs that can bounce light off the ceiling, creating the ambient layer.

Figure 20.4: Top: Four mounting details for linear LED lights on the top of structural beams. Bottom: To help avoid glare, mount track and directional luminaires on the sides of beams, not the bottoms.

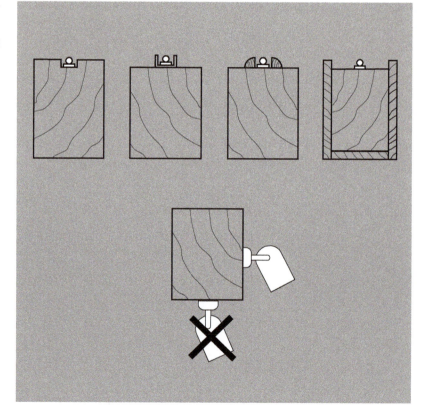

Cove Lighting

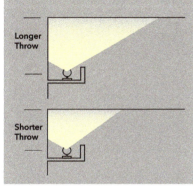
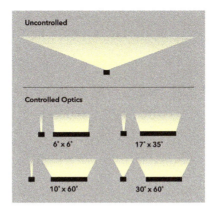

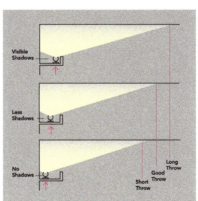

Figure 20.5: To design for the proper throw (distance from the wall), consider luminaire placement and optic type.

Figure 20.6: Linear LEDs with uncontrolled (or Lambertian) distribution have no optics to shape the beam. Many linear LEDs are available today with different combinations of the throw beam angle and the lateral beam angle, usually specified with two numbers, such as 10° x 60°.

Figure 20.7: For a longer throw of light on the ceiling, position the luminaire farther below the ceiling line.

Figure 20.8: Light will throw horizontally four times the distance the fixture is mounted from the ceiling line. The throw will vary if you use a controlled beam angle. The lip of the cover should be the height of the fixture and not higher, as this will also affect the throw of the light on the ceiling.

Figure 20.9: The lip of the cove should be flush with the top of the luminaire to hide the source from view while allowing the maximum amount of light out of the cove. Use a matte white interior finish inside of your cove and ceiling. Avoid shiny or reflective surfaces which can produce specular effects.

Figure 20.10: Within the cove, the closer you mount the fixture to the front edge, the farther your light will throw. However, the light will hit the back wall higher and you run the risk of getting a shadow line on your ceiling. The middle of the cove gives you a good throw and good coverage on the back wall. Placing the fixture on the back wall gives you less of a throw but no risk of a shadow line.

CHAPTER 20 Design Details 211

Wall Washing

Figure 20.11: For an even gradation from top to bottom, whether lighting from below or above, use luminaires with beam angles between 20–40°. Keep the luminaires relatively close to the wall for a better depth of structure.

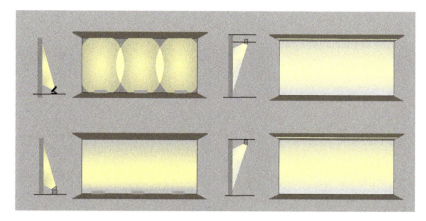

Figure 20.12: Movable uplights can provide a flexible solution for wall washing.

Figure 20.13: Uplights positioned behind plants wash the wall with light, providing visual interest with the strongly contrasting patterns of leaves.

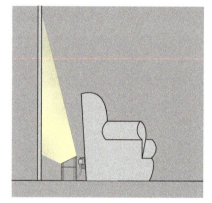

Wall Grazing

Figure 20.14: When uplighting, for a tighter beam, and more contrast on the wall surface, mount the luminaire closer to the wall. Conversely, the wider the optic, the farther away you should mount the luminaire.

Figure 20.15: Top: Placing the luminaire very close to the wall creates the most shadows with a sharp cutoff from the stones that protrude the furthest. Middle: A moderate setback results in less cutoff and shadows. Bottom: Placement far from the wall results in uniform illumination and minimal shadowing.

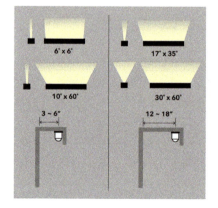
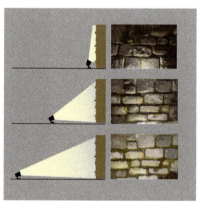

212 PART IV Design Details

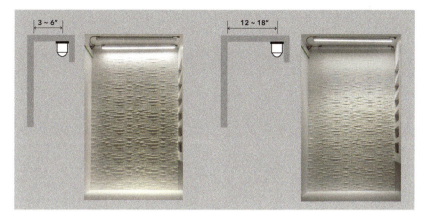

Figure 20.16: When downlighting, for a tighter beam and more dramatic contrast mount the luminaire closer to the wall. A beam with a wider spread should be mounted farther away from the wall and will produce less contrast. Photos: Courtesy of Ecosense.

Under-cabinet Lighting

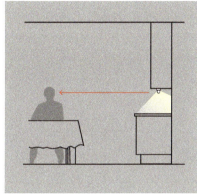

Figure 20.17: A linear LED task light mounted at the front of the cabinet bounces illumination off the backsplash and onto the countertop.

Figure 20.18: Be sure to shield under-cabinet luminaires from the direct eye level view of people sitting at kitchen tables or counters.

Pendants and Decorative Lighting

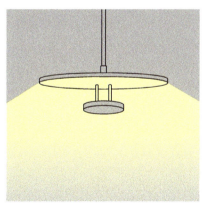

Figure 20.19: Using a torchière lamp is a fast, easy way of providing ambient light for a room.

Figure 20.20: This style of pendant luminaire reflects indirect light off a matte white disk to provide a soft glow.

Figure 20.21: Using only a chandelier in the center of the ceiling draws too much attention to itself and the rest of the room and the people are not illuminated properly.

Figure 20.22: Wall sconces provide the ambient light for the room, and also allow the chandelier to be dimmed so that it gives the illusion of providing the illumination without attracting too much attention to itself.

Figure 20.23: Torchières can also be a practical and easy way of adding ambient light. They provide the illumination that people will think comes from the chandelier, which can be dimmed to an appropriate level.

Skylights and Daylighting

Figure 20.24: During the day a pleated or Roman-type shade, or a fixed translucent shade fitted into the lightwell, will diffuse the daylight flooding into the room, reducing glare.

Figure 20.25: Skylights that diffuse daylight also serve as "lights" at night. Linear LEDs are mounted inside the lightwell and illuminate the translucent lens, providing a soft diffuse light and keeping the skylight form being a black hole at night.

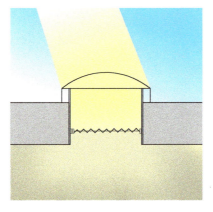

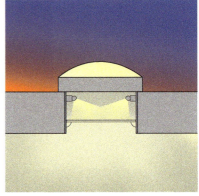

214 PART IV Design Details

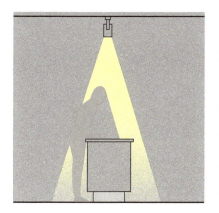
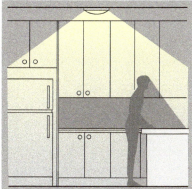

Downlights

Figure 20.26: Track lighting is a poor source of task light. People will be forced into working in their own shadows.

Figure 20.27: Work surfaces remain in shadow if the only light in a room is a surface-mounted luminaire in the center of the room.

Figure 20.28: Adjustable recessed downlights provide excellent accent cross lighting in place of a pendant luminaire.

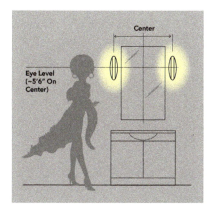
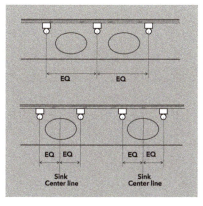

Vanity Lighting

Figure 20.29: Mount vanity lights at eye level, flanking the mirror, equidistant on center.

Figure 20.30: Two sinks mounted too far apart need a pair of light luminaires per sink. Two sinks mounted closer together can share three light luminaires.

CHAPTER 20 Design Details

Exterior Area and Security Lighting

Figure 20.31: A luminaire with clear or beveled glass shows off only the light bulb at night, creating blinding glare when guests approach the front door. Sandblasted or frosted panels soften the light and allow the luminaire itself to be the focal point.

Figure 20.32: For outdoor activity areas, luminaires placed above eye level provide efficient lighting for recreation, safety and security.

Figure 20.33: Forelighting the deck from under the eaves and uplighting the trees from under the deck will help make the outside feel like part of the interior spaces.

Figure 20.34: Decorative luminaires alone become too predominate, leaving the rest of the yard and house in relative darkness.

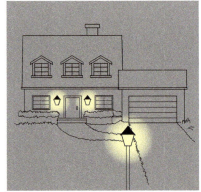

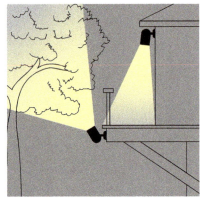

Landscape Lighting

Figure 20.35: Trees and shrubs with interesting branch structure are dramatic when silhouetted against a wall or building façade. This combination of landscape and façade lighting provides additional security near the building. Overlapping light patterns will soften shadows and create a more uniform lighting effect. Mount to trellises, gazebos, facades, eaves, or trees.

Figure 20.36: If the lighted object may be viewed from any direction, well lights are the ideal solution. These below-grade luminaires are louvered to further reduce the potential for glare. Use the optional directional louver to gain efficiency when the lamp must be tilted within the well.

Figure 20.37: When the lighted object can be viewed from one direction only, above-grade accent lights are the logical choice. To prevent direct glare, fixtures are aimed away from observers. Place the accent lights behind shrubbery to keep a natural looking landscape.

Figure 20.38: Moonlighting, the effect of moonlight filtering through trees, is a pleasing and functional outdoor lighting technique. Both uplights and downlights are used to create this effect. With luminaires properly placed in trees, both the trees and ground are beautifully illuminated. Ground lighting provides security, and is accented by shadows from leaves and branches.

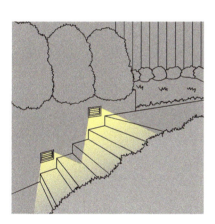

Path and Step Lights

Figure 20.39: Step lights can be mounted in the side walls of stair steps to provide safe illumination.

Figure 20.40: Fully shielded mushroom type lights highlight pathways and ground cover without drawing attention to themselves or creating distracting and potentially dangerous glare.

Part V | Resources

Glossary of Lighting Terms

These commonly used lighting terms are defined in plain English, so that homeowners, designers, and contractors can communicate more clearly.

Absorption
The amount of light which is absorbed by an object rather than being reflected. Dark colored and matte surfaces are least likely to reflect light.

Accent Lighting
Lighting directed at a particular object in order to focus attention upon it.

Ambient Lighting
The soft indirect light that fills the volume of a room. Ambient light softens shadows on people's faces and creates an inviting glow in the room.

Amperage
The amount of electrical current through a conductive source.

Angle of Reflectance
The angle at which a light source hits a specular reflective surface equals the angle at which the resulting glare is reflected back.

Beam Spread
The angle of the pattern of light produced by a lamp or luminaire.

Below Grade
Recessed below ground level.

Black Mirror Effect
Refers to an opening or window in a room that appears to be empty darkness, especially at night, because there is insufficient illumination at the other side to light up the objects or features framed by the opening.

Bridge System
Two wire, low voltage cable system.

Candela
The base unit of luminous intensity in the International System of Units (SI); that is, luminous power per unit solid angle emitted by a point light source in a particular direction.

Candlepower
An obsolete unit of measurement for luminous intensity. It expresses levels of light intensity relative to the light emitted by a candle of specific size and constituents.

Cold Cathode
A neon-like electric-discharge light source primarily used for illumination (neon is often used for signage or as an art form). Cold cathode can sometimes be used where fluorescent tubes would be too large or too hard to re-lamp.

Color Rendering Index (CRI)
A scale used to measure how well a lamp illuminates an object's color tones as compared with the color of a number of reference illuminants as defined by the CIE.

Cove Lighting
A technique for adding indirect (ambient) lighting into a space, where the light source is hidden by an architectural detail or a metal extrusion in the ceiling.

Decorative Luminaire
A luminaire designed to please the eye and provide focal illumination.

Derating
The reduction of the amount of wattage used to prevent overheating. Related to ganging of dimmers.

Diffusion Filters
Glass lenses used to widen, elongate or soften light output.

Dimmer
A control that regulates light levels on a smooth curve.

Dimming Ballast
Device used with fluorescent lamps to control the light level. May also apply to HID sources.

Driver
Device that regulates the voltage or current by changing it from AC to DC and monitoring voltage or current levels.

Efficacy
Measurement of the energy efficiency of a light source.

Elevation
Part of an architectural plan set that shows what vertical surfaces will look like.

ETL
An independent testing facility, similar to UL.

Fade Rate
Rate at which light levels decrease in controlled lighting.

Fiber optics
A illuminating system composed of a lamp source, fiber, and output optics used to remotely light an area or object.

Filters
Glass, plastic, or metal accessories attached to lamps or luminiares used to alter beam patterns or light color.

Fish Tape
A mechanical device used to pull wires in tight spaces or conduit.

Fluorescent Lamp
An efficient type of lamp that produces light through the activation of the phosphor coating on the inside surface of a glass envelope. These lamps come in may shapes, wattages, and colors.

Footcandle
A measurement of the total light reaching a surface, a non-SI unit of illuminance or light intensity. The footcandle is defined as one lumen per square foot.

Framing Projector
A luminaire that can be adjusted to precisely frame an object with light.

Ganging
Grouping two or more controls in one enclosure.

Glare/Glare Factor
A source of uncomfortably bright light that becomes the focus of attention rather than what it was meant to illuminate.

Halogen
An incandescent lamp containing halogen gas which recycles the tungsten.

Hard Wire
Method of luminaire installation using a junction box.

High Intensity Discharge (HID) Lamp
A category of lamp that emits light through electricity activating pressurized gas in a bulb. Mercury vapor, metal halide, and high pressure sodium lamps are all HID sources. They are bright, energy efficient, and quite ugly light sources used mainly in exterior environments.

Housing
Enclosure for recessed sockets and trim above the ceiling.

Incandescent Lamp
The old type of light bulb that produces light through electrical resistance causing a filament to glow. It is a very inefficient source of illumination.

Junction Box
An enclosure for joining wires behind walls or ceilings.

Kelvin
The base unit of temperature in the International System of Units, having the unit symbol K, also used as a measure of the color temperature of light.

Kilowatt
A thousand watts equals one kilowatt.

Lamp
What the lighting industry technically calls a light bulb. A glass envelope with gas, coating, or filament that glows when electrical current is applied. LED lamps are completely different from incandescents and don't need to be enclosed in glass bulbs, but are still referred to as "bulbs."

Line Voltage
The 110–120-volt household current, generally standard in North America.

Louver
A metal or plastic accessory used on a luminaire to help prevent glare.

Low-Voltage Lighting
System that uses less than 50-volt current (commonly 12-volt), instead of 110–120-volt, the standard household current. A transformer is used to convert the electrical power to the appropriate voltage.

Lumen
A unit of light power from a light source: the rate at which light falls on one square foot of surface area one foot away from a light source on one candlepower or on candela.

Lumen Maintenance
The measurement that determines the lifetime or useful light output rating of an LED light source. Unlike traditional light sources such as incandescent lamps, LEDs rarely fail outright and instead continue to emit light, albeit at slowly diminishing rate over time.

Luminaire
The complete light fixture with all parts and lamps (bulbs or LED components) necessary for positioning and obtaining power supply.

Luminous Flux
In photometry, luminous flux or luminous power is the measure of the perceived power of light.

Lux
Lux (symbol: lx) is the SI derived unit of illuminance, measuring luminous flux per unit area. It is equal to one lumen per square meter.

MR16 and MR11
Miniature tungsten halogen or LED lamps with a variety of beam spreads and wattages. MR stands for multifacted reflector.

Motion Sensor
A control which activates luminaires when movement occurs.

Neon
A glass vacuum tube filled with neon gas and phosphors formed into signs, letters or shapes.

Open Hearth Effect
Lighting that creates the feeling of a glowing fire.

Panic Switch
An on/off switch to activate security lighting, usually located by the bed for emergencies.

PAR (Parabolic Reflector) Lamps
Lamps (bulbs) with parabolic aluminized reflectors that give exacting beam control. There are a number of beam patterns to choose from, ranging from

wide flood to very narrow spot. PAR lamps can be used outdoors due to their thick glass, which holds up in severe weather conditions.

Photosensor
A control device that activates luminaires depending on surrounding light levels.

Radiant Flux
The measure of the total power of electromagnetic radiation (including infrared, ultraviolet, and visible light).

Swiss Cheese Effect
Too many holes in the ceiling from an overabundance of recessed fixtures. Also known as the Planetarium effect.

R Lamp
An incandescent source with a built-in reflecting surface.

Reflectance
The ratio of light reflected from a surface.

Reflected Ceiling Plan
A lighting plan drawn from the floor looking up at the ceiling above.

RLM Reflectors
A luminaire designed to reflect light down and prevent upward light transmission.

Spectral Power Distribution (SPD)
A measurement that describes the power per unit area per unit wavelength of an illumination (radiant exitance).

Spread Lens
A glass lenses accessory used to diffuse and widen beam patterns.

Stake Light
A luminaire mounted on a stake to go into the ground or a planter.

Switches
Controls for electrical devices, including lights and luminaires.

Task Lighting
Illumination designed for a work surface free of shadows and glare.

Timers
Control devices to activate luminaires at set timed intervals.

TM-30
Refers to the Illuminating Engineering Society's Technical Memorandum 30-15 IES Method for Evaluating Light Source Color Rendition.

Transformer
A device which can raise or lower electrical voltage, generally used for low voltage lights.

Tungsten-Halogen
A tungsten incandescent lamp (bulb) which contains gas and burns hotter and brighter than standard incandescent lamps.

UL
Underwriters Laboratory, an independent testing company.

Veiling Reflection
A mirror like reflection of a bright source on a shiny surface.

Voltage
A measurement of the pressure of electricity going through a wire.

Voltage Drop
The decrease of light output in fixtures further from the transformer in low voltage lighting systems.

White Light
Usually refers to light with a color temperature between 5000–6250 degrees Kelvin and composed of the whole visible light spectrum. This light allows all colors in the spectrum on an object's surface to be reflected, providing good color-rendering qualities. Daylight is the most commonly referred to source of white light.

Xenon
An inert gas used as a component in certain incandescent lamps to produce a cooler color temperature than standard incandescent. It is often used in applications where halogen may normally be specified, because of a longer lamp life.

Bibliography

The following sources have provided inspiration and illuminating ideas in our quest for *Beautiful Light*.

The Structure of Light: Richard Kelly and the Illumination of Modern Architecture
Dietrich Neumann and Robert A.M. Stern, Yale University Press, Illustrated Edition (January 25, 2011)
SBN-10: 0300163703 ISBN-13: 978-0300163704

L.E.D.: A History of the Future of Lighting
Bob Johnstone, CreateSpace Independent Publishing Platform; 1st Edition (May 19, 2017)
SBN-10: 1546737421 ISBN-13: 978-1546737421

Empires of Light: Edison, Tesla, Westinghouse, and the Race to Electrify the World
Jill Jonnes, Random House Trade Paperbacks (October 12, 2004)
ISBN-10: 0375758844 ISBN-13: 978-0375758843

Brilliant: The Evolution of Artificial Light
Jane Brox, Mariner Books; 1st Edition (June 29, 2010)
ASIN: B003U4VESK

Tesla, Inventor of the Electrical Age
W. Bernard Carlson, Princeton University Press; Reprint edition (April 27, 2015)
ISBN-10: 0691165610 ISBN-13: 978-0691165615

Office for Visual Interaction: Lighting Design and Process
Wolfgang Neumann, Jovis (May 31, 2014)
ISBN-10: 3868592563 ISBN-13: 978-3868592566

Color and Light: Luminous Atmospheres for Painted Rooms
Donald Kaufman, Taffy Dahl, Christine Pittel, Dominique Vorillon, Clarkson Potter; 1st Edition (April 27, 1999)
ISBN-10: 0517704013 ISBN-13: 978-0517704011

Electrifying America: Social Meanings of a New Technology, 1880–1940
David E. Nye, The MIT Press; Reprint edition (July 8, 1992)
ISBN-13: 978-0262640305 ISBN-10: 0262640309

A Syllabus of Stage Lighting
Stanley McCandless, Drama Book Specialists [11th ed.] Edition (January 1, 1964)
ASIN: B0006D01GY

Brilliant!: Shuji Nakamura And the Revolution in Lighting Technology
Bob Johnstone, Prometheus; Updated Edition (February 3, 2015)
ISBN-10: 1633880621 ISBN-13: 978-1633880627

Residential Lighting Guide for 2019 Building Energy Efficiency Standards
Nicole Hathaway, LC, Adrian Ang, Michael Siminovitch, PhD., California Lighting Technology Center, University of California, Davis, Available at https://cltc.ucdavis.edu

Acknowledgments

We would like to thank all the photographers, designers, and architects who contributed their inspiring work to this book. These fine images of their projects show how well-done lighting can be integrated seamlessly into interior and exterior environments. Our job in this book is to pull back the curtain and reveal the design process behind the finished product. Without them, this would not have been possible.

Our appreciation goes out to designers John Martin of Turner Martin Design, Kristi Will of Kristi Will Home + Design, and Alfredo Zaparolli of Techlinea who have all been frequent collaborators over the years. Special thanks is due to Chris Smith-Peterson of Ecosense, who stands out in the industry as a gifted educator and passionate lighting expert, for his help and collaboration in the material on linear LEDs, and to Paul Pickard of Ecosense, one of the top minds in lighting today. We also thank our excellent friends and colleagues Jim Benya, Naomi Miller, and Jan Moyer for their thoughtful answers to last-minute questions.

Also, our deepest gratitude goes to the marvelous photographers who know how to capture the magic of light in their images. Among the best are Dennis Anderson, Russell Abraham, and Misha Bruk. Lighting design is a visual medium. We need photographs to tell the story of illumination, and photographing lighting to convey the experience in the environment is a great art that requires the ability to see and communicate on a different level. Light is not something you can hold; it is something that you feel. We are grateful to the publishers and editors at Routledge for allowing us to use as many pictures we believed were needed to tell the story.

We would also like to thank the lighting companies Soraa, Ecosense, and Bridgelux, who granted us permission to use many of the graphs, charts, and illustrations included in the book. And finally, thanks to lighting designer, Callie Welsh, who graciously agreed to be our model for the shots on pages 31 and 33.

All of these contributors understand the importance of teaching the fundamentals of lighting design to students of interior design, architecture, lighting design, and landscape design. Homeowners also need a guidebook to assist them in selecting the right fixtures and components, and in speaking more confidently to their designers and contractors about what they want.

Thank you all.

Randall Whitehead
Clifton Stanley Lemon

Index

Note: References in *italics* are to figures; 'g' refers to the glossary:

A-lamps 53
absorption 222g
accent lighting 34, *35*, 36, *37*, *39*, 51, 222g; bathrooms 96; dining rooms 124, 125, 132; exterior spaces 184, 186, *187*, 188; living rooms 118, *119*
ambient lighting 31, 34, *35*, 36, *37*, 40, 222g; bathrooms 96; bedrooms 138; dining rooms 124–125; exterior spaces 184, 188, *189*; open plan spaces 168–170, *169*, *171*
amperage 222g
angle of reflectance 222g
area lights 51
Average Spectral Difference (ASD) *27*

B-10 lamps 53
Baker, Alex 15
bathrooms 8, 94, *95*, *97*, *106*, *107*; 1 guest bath 98, *99*; 2 master bath 100, *101*; 3 integrated lighting 102, *103*; 4 master bath 104, *105*; accent lighting 96; ambient lighting 96; lighting for tubs and showers 96
beam spread 222g
bedrooms 138, *139*, 140; 1 guest bedroom 142, *143*; 2 master bedroom 144, *145*; 3 sumptuous rooms 146, *147*; 4 master bedroom 148, *149*; ambient lighting 138; ceiling luminaires 148, *150*; closets 140, *141*, *151*; task lighting 138, 140
below-grade luminaires 216, 220g
"black mirror" effect 84, 114, 160, 184, 186, 198, 222g
BR (Bulb Reflector) lamp 52–53
bridge systems 170, 222g
Bridgelux *27*
brightness 22–23, *23*

candela 222g
candlepower 222g
candles 12, *18*, 125, *127*, *137*

CCT (Correlated Color Temperature) 4, 16, 24–26, *25*, *26*, 33, *33*, 42, 44, 45, 56, 76, *76*, 77
ceilings 36, 50, *210*; bedrooms 148, *150*; dining rooms 128, *129*; living rooms 108, 110, 116, *117*; reflected ceiling plans 226g
CFLs (compact fluorescents) 2, 14
chandeliers 50, *54*, 122, *123*, 126, 130, *131*, *136*
cold cathode 223g
color 42; and food *43*, 44, 45; in kitchens 82; local color 42; three approaches 45–46, *46*, *47*
color rendering 2, 4, 16, *26*, 26–28, *27*, *28*, 31–33, *32*, 42, 45
Color Rendering Index (CRI) 2, 4, 16, *26*, 26, 44, 223g
color temperature *see* CCT (Correlated Color Temperature)
color tuning 16, 16–17, *17*, *38*
compact fluorescents (CFLs) 2, 14
controls 56, 126; basic needs 56–57; dimmers 18, *55*, 56–57, 114, 118, 126, 176, 223g; occupancy sensors 57; scenes 57, *59*; smart lighting, smart home 57–58; vacancy sensors 57
Correlated Color Temperature *see* CCT (Correlated Color Temperature)
cove lighting 36, 37, *39*, 138, *211*, 223g
CRI *see* Color Rendering Index

daylighting *214*
decorative lighting: exterior spaces 184, 188; open plan spaces *169*, 170
decorative luminaires 34, *35*, *37*, *213–214*, 223g; dining rooms 65, 122, 124–125, 132, 134; entries 152; exterior lighting 52, 184, 188, *216*; kitchens 80, 88; living rooms 118; open plan spaces *169*, 170, 174, 178
derating 223g
design details 218, *209*; ceilings *210*; cove lighting *211*; daylighting

214; decorative lighting *213–214*; downlights *215*; exterior area *216*; landscape lighting *216–217*; path and step lights *217*; pendants *213–214*; security lighting *216*; skylights *214*; under-cabinet lighting *213*; vanity lighting *215*; wall grazing *212–213*; wall washing *212*
design process: collaboration 64; information gathering 64–65; meeting with clients 66, *66*; renderings and mockups 65–66, *66*, *67*; testing ideas 65–66
diffusion filters 223g
dimmers and dimming 18, *55*, 56–57, 114, 118, 126, 176, 223g
dimming ballast 223g
dining rooms 122, 126; 1 high ceilings 128, *129*; 2 drama 130, *131*; 3 transitional design 132, *133*; 4 Asian fusion 134, *135*; accent layer 124, 125, 132; ambient layer 124–125; candles 125, *127*, *137*; chandeliers 122, *123*, 126, 130, *131*, *136*; controls 126; light layering 126, *136*; size and positioning 65, 124
direction of light 24, *24*, 31
directional lamps 52–53
downlights 30, *31*, 37, *38*, 49, 176, *215*; recessed 46, 49, 94, 130, 134, 140, 156, *157*, 164
drivers 223g

efficacy 223g
Eichler, Joseph 168
electric lighting 12
elevation 223g
energy codes for lighting 60, 62
entries 152, *166*, *167*; 1 impact *153*, 156, *157*, 205; 2 art gallery 158–160, *159*, *161*; 3 spiral staircase 162, *163*; 4 What's wrong with this picture? 164, *165*; light layering 154, *155*; size matters 152, *153*
ETL 223g
exterior luminaires *39*, 51–52, 188, 190, *198*, *199*
exterior spaces 184, *185*, 204–205, *216*; 1 Balinese teahouse 192, *193*, *194*, *195*; 2 sense of presence 196, *197*; 3 garden luminaires 198, *199*; 4 alfresco living 200, *201*; 5 desert landscaping 202, *203*; accent layer 184, *186*, *187*, 188; ambient layer 184, 188, *189*; color and output 190; decorative layer 184, 188; exterior ratings 190; size and whispers 188; street smart 186, *187*; task layer 184, 186, *187*

fade rate 57, 223g
fiber optics 223g
filters 223g
fire line theory of lighting 13
fish tape 224g
flame-tip lamps 53
floor lamps 2, 49; bedrooms 138, 148; dining rooms 125; entries 154, 156, 164; living rooms 114, 118; open plan spaces 170, 172
fluorescent lamps 1, 224g; compact fluorescents (CFLs) 2, 14; light distribution 18, *18*; light production 19, *19*
footcandles 23, 224g
framing projectors 224g

ganging 224g
gas lamps 12
glare/glare factor 224g
glass, development of 12
Glossary 222–227g
great rooms *see* open plan spaces

halogens 2, 14, 16, 224g
hard wire 224g
high intensity discharge (HID) lamps 224g
"home" 10, *11*
horizontal surfaces 36
housing 49, 224g
human-centric design 8

Illuminating Engineering Society (IES) 15, 27
incandescent lamps 1, 2, 14, 224g; color rendering 16, 42; light distribution 18, *18*; light production 19, *19*
inground lights 51
intensity of light 22–23, *23*
interior lighting 78; bathrooms 94–107; bedrooms 138–151; dining rooms 122–137; entries 152–167; evolution of 10–12, *11*; kitchens 80–93; living rooms 108–121; open plan spaces 168–181
interior luminaires 49–50

junction boxes 224g

230　　　　　　　　　　　　　　　　　　　　　　　　　　　INDEX

K (Kelvin) 4, 25, 224g
Kelly, Richard 12
kerosene lamps 12
kilowatts 224g
kitchens 80–82, *81*, *83*, *93*; 1 transitional style 84, *85*; 2 contemporary style 86, *87*; 3 desert design 88, *89*; 4 spacious kitchen 90, *91*; blend without blending 80; color me comfortable 82; galley kitchen *92*; open plan 78, 82, 168; under-cabinet lighting 65, 70, 71, 82, 84, 86, 88, 90, *213*

lamps 2, 14, 224g; directional lamps 52–53; "integrated" luminaires 48; interior luminaires 49–50; with luminaires 48; omnidirectional lamps 53; quality of light 48
landscape lighting *216–217*
LEDs (light emitting diodes) 1, 2, 8, 12, 14, *54*; color rendering 16; color temperature 16; color tuning 16, 16–17, *17*, *38*; dimming and warm dimming 18, 56–57; energy efficiency 14–15, 60; flexibility and size 15; form 15; light distribution 18, *18*, 23; light production *19*, 19–20, *20*; linear LED lighting 50, *54*, *55*; longevity and maintenance 15; thermal performance 16
light bulbs *see* lamps
light distribution 18, *18*, 23
light layering 1, 12, *13*, 34–36, *35*, *37*, *38*, *40*; decorative, accent, task 110; dining rooms 126, *136*; entries 154, *155*; horizontal surfaces 36; outdoors *39*; vertical surfaces 36, *37*
light production *19*, 19–20, *20*
light qualities 22, 48; color rendering 26, 26–28, *27*, *28*; color temperature 24–26, *25*, *26*; direction 24, *24*, 31; distribution 18, *18*, 23; intensity 22–23, *23*; local color 42; movement 28, *29*
lighting fails 8, 68–69, *69*; drama queen entry 75, *75*; Euro-posing 70, *70*; not quite there yet 74, *74*; poor CCT/lack of focus 76, *76*; single bulbs 72, *72*; specular reflections 71, *71*; Swiss cheese ceilings 37, 73, *73*, 226g
lighting people *see* people, lighting of
line voltage 225g

linear LED lighting 50, *54*, *55*
living rooms 108, *109*, *120*, *121*; 1 art collection 112, *113*; 2 alluring retreat 114, *115*; 3 high ceilings 108, 110, 116, *117*; 4 accent lighting 118, *119*; uplight and out of sight 110, *111*
louvers 225g
low-voltage lighting 225g
lumen maintenance 15, 225g
lumens 23, 225g
lumens per Watt (lm/W) 14–15
luminaires 2, 225g; below grade 216, 222g; ceiling luminaires 148, *150*; exterior luminaires *39*, 51–52, 188, 190, 198, *199*; integrated luminaires 48; interior luminaires 49–50; quality of light 48; with replaceable lamps 48; *see also* decorative luminaires
luminous flux 225g
lux (lx) 23, 225g

materials 42, *43*, *44*
Maurer, Ingo 112, 116
McCandless, Stanley 23, 30
motion sensors 186, 225g
MR16/MR11 (Multifaceted Reflectors) 14, 52, 225g

neon 223, 225g

occupancy sensors 57
oil lamps 12
omnidirectional lamps 53
open hearth effect 225g
open plan spaces 78, 108, 168, *180*, *181*; 1 condominium 172, *173*; 2 living/dining room 174, *175*; 3 outdoor rooms 176, *177*; 4 defined spaces 178, *179*; ambient light layer 168–170, *169*, *171*; decorative layer *169*, 170; kitchens 78, 82, 168
outdoor lights *see* exterior luminaires

panic switches 225g
PAR (Parabolic Aluminized Reflectors) 14, 52, 225–226g
path lights 51, *217*
pendants 50, *54*, *55*, 128, *129*, *213–214*
people, lighting of 8, 12, 24, 30, *31*, 78, 138; color rendering 31–33, *32*; color temperature 33, *33*; direction and balance 31; skin 8, *28*, 31–33, *32*, 98, 138

photosensors 226g
Popcorn, Faith 122

R lamps 224g
radiant flux 224g
reflectance 224g; angle of reflectance 222g
reflected ceiling plans 226g
reveals 38
RLM reflectors 226g

scenes 57, *59*
security lighting 58, 186, *216*, *217*, 225
single bulbs 72, *73*
skin 8, *28*, 31–33, *32*, 98, 138
skylights 162, 178, *214*
skyline/fire line theory of lighting *13*
smart lighting, smart home 57–58
solid state lighting *see* LEDs (light emitting diodes)
spectral power distribution (SPD) 226g
specular reflections 71, *71*
Spira, Joel 56
spread lenses 226g
stage lighting 30
stake lights 226g
step lights 51, *217*
sustainable design 60; basic requirements 60, 62; efficiency is beautiful 62; energy codes for lighting 60, 62; importance of 60
Swiss cheese effect 37, 73, *73*, 226g
switches 56, 118, 176, 198, 226g; panic switches 225g; vacancy sensors 57; *see also* dimmers and dimming

table lamps 49
task lighting 34, *35*, *37*, 110, 226g; bedrooms 138, 140; exterior spaces 184, 186, *187*
terminology 2–3, 222–227g
timers 226g
TM-30 27, *27*, 226g
track and rail systems 49
transformers 102, 226g
tunable color *16*, 16–17, *17*
tungsten-halogen 227g

UL (Underwriters Laboratory) 227g
under-cabinet lighting 65, 70, 71, 82, 84, 86, 88, 90, *213*
uplights 51

V (volts) 4
vacancy sensors 57
vanity lighting 8, 31, 50, 96, 98, *99*, *215*
veiling reflection 227g
vertical surfaces (lighting of) 36, 37
vision 10
voltage 227g; line voltage 225g; low-voltage lighting 225g
voltage drop 227g

W (Watts) 4
wall grazing 37, *39*, *212–213*
wall lights 50
wall washing 37, *38*, *212*
warm dimming 18
well lights 51
white light 19, 20, 227g
windows 12; *see also* "black mirror" effect

xenon 225g